CALL ME COACH
TEAM SPORTS AND LIFE

iUniverse books may be ordered through booksellers or by contacting:

iUniverse
1663 Liberty Drive
Bloomington, IN 47403
www.iuniverse.com
1-800-Authors (1-800-288-4677)

ISBN: 978-1-5320-4621-6 (sc)
ISBN: 978-1-5320-4620-9 (e)

Library of Congress Control Number: 2018905995

Print information available on the last page.

iUniverse rev. date: 07/11/2018

To the late Perry Reese Jr., a Highland High School history teacher and state championship basketball coach who touched lives. As Perry often said, "Call me Coach."

CONTENTS

- Develop a Playbook
- Ball Exchange
- Blocking Scheme
- Play Area
- Personnel
- Play-Series Consistency
- Post-snap Reads
- Offensive Tactical Options
- Defensive Tactical Options
- Implement Strategy and Tactics
- Offensive-Plan Priorities
- Defensive-Plan Priorities
- Special-Situations Priorities

- Practice Schedule
- Turning Around a Losing Team
- Thoughts for a New Coach
- Scouting
- Offensive Scouting Information
- Defensive Scouting Information
- Special Teams Scouting Information
- Game Day

- The Lure of Team Sports

ACKNOWLEDGMENTS

To my first wife, Ellen; my second wife, Kathy Lou; and my sister-in-law Gretchen Givens, for teaching me to have passion for what I do. As Kathy Lou always told her actors, "You better sparkle!"

I was fortunate to play for and coach with Lawrence "Art" Teynor, who was the head football coach at Dover St. Joseph/Tuscarawas Central Catholic (Ohio) for thirty-five years. He had five undefeated seasons and eight one-loss seasons, with teams rated in the UPI top ten twelve different years. He was named AP's Eastern District Coach of the Year seven times and was the National High School Ohio athletic director in 1985.

To Perry Reese Jr., who was a total coach, from providing his players with state championship–level competition to being liked and respected by his peers and his community. He was a black athlete at Canton South High School who found his home in the Amish country of Holmes County, Ohio, and his name is now on the high school gymnasium. Perry's greatest gift was teaching us about love—love for his players, love for the game, and love for his profession.

To my friends in the Losers' Club who taught me the most important lesson in life: it's not about winning; it's about how you play the game to win. And to Wally Morton, lifelong president of the Losers' Club, who is now in the Greater Cleveland Sports Hall of Fame after thirty-seven years as the men's swim coach at Cleveland State University.

ABOUT THE AUTHOR

Glenn Myers was born and raised in the center of Ohio's football history, within an easy drive of the Pro Football Hall of Fame and high school powerhouses such as Massillon and Canton McKinley. He took a college class on coaching high school football that was taught by the late Bill Hess, who took an 0–10 Ohio University team to a 10–0 regular season with a Tangerine Bowl appearance three years later. Myers has remained a student of the game ever since.

As a school psychologist, Myers served large and small school systems; a preschool that taught children to overcome the challenges of being blind, deaf, or physically restricted by congenital conditions or injuries; and a diagnostic team of medical and educational specialists for multiple handicapped students aged six months to twenty-six years.

He has applied his experiences in educational psychology to sports through coaching, officiating, and studying youth-league experiences in most team sports, and he has spent a lifetime of learning and play in sport activities from shooting, skiing, and sailing to a full range of team sports.

His thirty-four-year career as a trial attorney adds training and experience in writing, teaching, and strategic thinking that helps him provide an in-depth course in the steps to successful team-sport coaching.

or dude ranch, or the operation of corporations, partnerships, or homeowners' associations, my life as a trial attorney was a life of study. From my early sports experiences as a player and coach to my study of team sports from the point of view of the players, parents, and volunteer coaches, I've studied how coaching works and why many coaches are not successful.

As I've listened to, read about, and observed successful coaches and watched those who fall short of the pinnacle, I've seen the same combination of traits as those presented by the corporate executives with whom I worked as a commercial trial attorney for thirty-four years. Using a corporate model is valid because successful coaching is now big business. Salaries and budgets for team-sport programs rival large corporations, and coaches spend much more time in the office than they do on the field.

My background in school psychology, especially working with children who had to overcome physical and emotional challenges to find success, provided a framework for the essence of coaching: the bond of love and trust that brings forth the best in every player.

Phil Jackson was a two-time NBA championship coach with the Los Angeles Lakers and the Chicago Bulls. He is now a board member and national spokesperson of the Positive Coaching Alliance, a national organization whose mission is "to transform the youth sports culture into a Developmental Zone where all youth and high school athletes have a positive, character-building experience that results in better athletes, better people."[1] As demonstrated by Phil Jackson, providing a quality experience for athletes is accomplished by the coach.

THE ANSWER

Victories identify those good coaches who have mastered the roles of a total coach. Attempting to identify or define the qualities of a successful coach is difficult because the keys to success are an array of personal habits and skills combined in the unique personality of

---

[1] "Mission Statement," Positive Coaching Alliance, accessed October 3, 2017, http://www.positivecoach.org/about/mission statement.

each coach. The one common trait of successful coaches is that they love what they do and are passionate about how they do it. Being a coach is not a single role; it is a combination of many roles that infuse every aspect of team sports:

- **teacher**, of subjects from how to catch a ball to how to live a rewarding life
- **parent**, acting *in loco parentis* (in place of the parents) to provide safety, moral development, and love
- **leader**, by organization, goal setting, decision-making, and example; a planner of everything involving the program, including competitive strategy
- **communicator**, to implement a personal vision for the program

Understanding the roles assumed by successful coaches provides the foundation for expressing the personal values and goals that make each coach unique. The how-to answer is not in doing it the way others do it; it is in knowing what to do in a way that is true to yourself. *Call Me Coach* provides a program for achieving a personal coaching style that will return all the magic of team-sports success, including the satisfaction of providing a rewarding and life-changing experience to every player you touch.

Success in any sport starts with knowledge of the subject. In this book I explain what coaches should know about their profession to be effective coaches. I discuss how to teach sports subjects to a team of players in chapter 2, "Becoming a Teacher," which summarizes learning theory and educational psychology. I address how to become a successful leader in chapter 3 by using my own experiences and the words of true leaders who are recognized not only for their success but also for the type of people they are. A sport program is the day-to-day expression of the coach's personal vision, and a personal management/leadership style is the means to achieving that vision.

Very few books and products for coaching team sports address an essential element of success—strategic thinking. To understand and embrace strategic thinking, it is necessary to learn from military strategy and intelligence, game theory, risk management, and philosophy. Applying strategic thinking to team sports involves a cohesive strategic system, taught and perfected in practice and executed against specific opponents. In this book I use football as the example for sports strategy because the number of players and the play-by-play nature of the game provide the most detailed review of strategic and tactical issues. However, most team sports require the same strategic approach to developing and executing a successful style of play. Strategy should guide every aspect of a team-sport program, from the use of available player talent to the player-position techniques taught in practice to the application of scouting information in making a game plan for tactical adjustments.

The final expression of a coach's vision is the experience he or she provides to the players, from practice sessions to shared planning and goals to individual and team success. In chapter 5, "Practice Defines Play," I reveal the coaching techniques that can create the atmosphere needed to bring forth the full value of sportsmanship, personal growth, and shared success available in team sports.

Developing the essential skills of a total coach in the context of the unique and complex world of coaching is a process of self-analysis and personal growth, leading to the interpersonal relationships and self-expression that embody the role of a coach and that explain why true coaches retain that title of respect for all their lives.

The available books containing "secrets of success" in life have one thing in common—positive, purposeful change. If you are not already successful, then you need to change to become successful—change the way you do things and who you are. The present situation does not determine where you go, only where you start. *Call Me Coach* is your path to the coach you want to become.

Because of the scope of information essential to successful coaching, I present the material as a textbook to support a college-level course that addresses all eight domains of the National Standards for Sport Coaches promulgated by the Society of Health and Physical Educators (SHAPE). On the whole, however, the book is not academic but rather a user-friendly guide for both new coaches and experienced coaches who are looking for the keys to success. I present the covered topics as a developmental continuum starting with the basics for a single, first-time coach with first-time players and ending with the advanced concepts found in major high school and college programs. An annotated bibliography provides suggestions for beginning and advanced study of the subjects discussed herein, and an appendix of both digital and organizational resources contains an outline of the professional support that is readily available to all coaches.

slogan 'Press On' has solved and always will solve the problems of the human race."[2]

- *Organization*—Successful people see the big picture in the smallest of details. In physics, chaos theory suggests that even the most random, disorganized activity has an underlying pattern of organization. Some people appear very organized because they see things from the bottom up, starting with the details. This is called inductive reasoning—working from the details to get to the big picture. Other people appear scattered and disorganized because they see the big picture and let the details fall into place—deductive reasoning, working from the top down. Whether you think from the bottom or the top, it is important to see the forest and not the trees.
- *Passion*—Having passion is about loving what you do and being present in every moment.
- *Confidence*—Confident people are courageous in the face of challenges. Henry Ford, a leader, an inventor, and the founder of the Ford Motor Company, captured the essence of positive thinking when he said, "Whether you think you can or you can't, you're probably right."
- *Efficiency*—Everyone's time is precious, and time is the key in every race.
- *Compassion*—Above all else, a coach must care for the players. Even at the highest levels of competitive professional sports, the coach-player relationship is the foundation for success. The goal is to connect with every player on the team, and this goal is achieved by placing each player's safety above your goals as coach, treating each player as an individual, and living the values you expect your players to learn. The connection for coaches, especially with younger players, is to see life and the sport as the players see it. You should strive to meet them on their level of experience and emotional development, listen to what they say, and provide the

---

[2] Leo Hand, *Defensive Coordinator's Football Handbook* (Monterey, CA: Coaches Choice, 2015), 226.

personal help they are asking for, not the help you think they need.

No one is born a successful coach or even born with the skills and traits necessary for success. You do not become a good coach by reading a book or by taking a class. There is no static checklist or formula that will work for everyone. Rather, the key lies in personal growth and development, for as we see in the wide variety of personalities of acclaimed coaches, each one is his or her own person, comfortable in the way he or she has chosen to master the art and science of coaching.

The journey of personal growth and development begins with an awareness of your life philosophy. We all have a belief system, developed by our parents, teachers, and experiences as we matured, but not many of us look inward to understand the basis of those beliefs. Part of living in the present moment is seeing that moment without the old filters and judgments from the past. (I have known people who never go back to great places because subsequent visits are never as good as the first visit.) Being aware of our beliefs requires an analysis of how we perceive the world and how we bring expectations and possible prejudgments to our experiences.

One way to look at our own beliefs is in the context of how they are reflected in long-established values to live by. A personal philosophy of life is not dependent on religion, faith, or classical philosophy, because virtually all major religions and many philosophies share the same basic tenets, such as the golden rule, belief in a higher power, and an afterlife. The life you choose in your everyday moments can be guided by a set of widely accepted principles that are held by most successful people. Here are some concepts to keep in mind.

LIVE IN THE PRESENT MOMENT

Every moment is exactly as it should be, whether it seems like it or not. Do not judge; just accept what is, and find contentment in the experiences life provides. Life happens in the present; it does not happen in memories of the past or hopes for the future.

Phil Jackson, who stood out as a professional coach because he was comfortable talking about sports in the context of these higher personal values, said, "In basketball—as in life—true joy comes from being fully present in each and every moment, not just when things are going your way. Of course, it's no accident that things are more likely to go your way when you stop worrying about whether you're going to win or lose and focus your full attention on what's happening right this moment."[3]

LIVE FOR YOURSELF

Always take the high road, and stay true to what you know is right. Whenever you are not sure about something, listen to your inner self. The path to peace and confidence is not found in the opinions of others.

CHALLENGE THE MYTHS

S. C. Gwynne's *The Perfect Pass: American Genius and the Reinvention of Football* tells the story of an obscure coach who pursued his dream offense after he lost his position as a quarterback and receivers coach at West Texas State University. To develop his offense he became the head football coach at Copperas Cove High School in Texas and then became head football coach for a team at Iowa Wesleyan College that had six players, no uniforms, and no game field. These were the only programs in the country where he could run his "air-raid" passing offense, because it was too different from the systems that successful programs were using. The coach was Hal Mumme, and he and an assistant coach, a former lawyer named Mike Leach, perfected the air-raid offense and set records wherever they coached. Mike Leach is now the head football coach at Washington State University, and his team just upset fourth-ranked Southern Cal early in the 2017 season.

An important lesson from this story is that there is no one "right

---

[3] Hand, *Defensive Coordinator's Football Handbook*, 230.

way" to do anything in sports. For example, P. J. Fleck, former successful coach at Western Michigan University and now head football coach at the University of Minnesota, changed the way ball carriers hold the ball, adding a fifth point of contact with the body to reduce the number of fumbles. Follow your instincts and question the way all the successful programs are doing things, from the amount of player-to-player contact in practice to strategy and tactics for game situations.

LIVE AS A STUDENT

One of the key personal habits to being successful and growing into the role of a total coach is a desire to be a student and to learn something new every day. Live as if you were going to die tomorrow, but learn as if you were going to live forever.

Every experience in life, good or bad, is a lesson—a lesson about old fears, about prejudging, about new ways to do things. Always question. Ask yourself things like "How do I help this player overcome …?" and "Why is this play not working?" and "How should I deal with bad calls from the officials?" When the student is ready, the teacher will appear. Everyone you meet may be a teacher to help answer your questions or show you a new lesson, but you'll never know how that will happen if you do not ask the questions. You will be amazed at what appears for you when you live as a student.

Many of the biographies of successful coaches discuss the fellowship that exists within the coaching profession. Professional coaches regularly share their time and ideas with college coaches, and college coaches open their practices to high school coaches. The off-season is filled with clinics, seminars, and camps for coaches to learn and share with other coaches. The depth of this coaching fellowship is presented in the movie *We Are Marshall*, about the true-story attempts of West Virginia's Marshall University to rebuild its football program after virtually its entire team and coaching staff were lost in a plane crash. In the movie, a new coach, with a new staff and players no one else wanted, searches for a strategic system to make them competitive. He visits Bobby Bowden, the head coach of West Virginia University (later to become a championship-level coach at Florida State University), to ask for Coach Bowden's entire offensive system. Without hesitation, Coach Bowden opens his playbook and film room for whatever Marshall needs.

FOCUS ON YOUR GOALS

Set clear goals for every aspect of your life, and then live every day in moving toward your goals. Do the same for your team. The path and opportunities will appear for you. There are no setbacks, only lessons. Think of the common story about Thomas Edison, the inventor of the lightbulb, who viewed each failure as a lesson that taught him another way not to make a lightbulb.

BECOME A LEADER

Lead, follow, or get out of the way. Many professionals have a choice of whether to assume leadership responsibility as part of their personal development. Coaches do not. The essence of coaching is fully committed, full-time leadership.

Becoming an effective leader requires an understanding of interpersonal dynamics and the development of essential leadership skills. The starting point is to be yourself. If you are calm and quiet, do not try to become loud and volatile. If you charge into every experience, do not give up your energy. Each outstanding leader is living a personal style and philosophy. Decide what kind of person you want to become, and then be that person in every aspect of your coaching, from teaching to strategizing to forming relationships with every player. When you are in doubt about a situation or the path to follow, find model leaders whose style and philosophy are compatible with yours, and then learn from them.

It is helpful to remember that to lead a parade, you must get in front of where the parade is going. Coaches learn where the team is going by helping players set goals for themselves and the team.

This process is the connection that forms the bond of leadership. The goals a team may choose arise from the personal qualities a coach presents in his or her interaction with players. Do not expect a team to become something you are not.

CHAPTER 2
BECOME A TEACHER

THE SUCCESS OF FAMILIES AND SOCIETIES LIES IN THE ABILITY TO PASS ON KNOWLEDGE.

A critical skill of successful coaches is the ability to teach, because coaches are required to teach a range of distinct subjects from life skills to one-on-one defense. A total coach must also understand the teaching role in the context of the different students involved in a team sport. Teaching is an art and a science. The science is centered in learning theory, how people learn. The art involves using appropriate teaching techniques in the context of interpersonal relationships, both individual and group. A total coach must master the sport subjects, understand how each of the students learns best, and then use the appropriate techniques to efficiently achieve the program goals.

TEAM-SPORT STUDENTS

A classroom teacher typically teaches a specific subject to a group of pupils of the same grade level. A coach, on the other hand, is presented with a wide variety of pupils—assistant coaches and volunteers; players of varying age, experience, and skill levels; parents and boosters, who should be educated about the program; and, most importantly, a team that changes every season. A coach must teach each of these student groups a range of different subjects.

Assistant Coaches

Whether paid or volunteers, assistants appear with varying levels of knowledge and experience about their roles as coaches, teachers, and strategists. These are important students because they will work in partnership with the coach to teach the system and skills the coach has chosen for the program. The more educated the assistants, the more they can contribute to the program.

The Players

The players are obvious students, but they present a diverse mix of sport experience, maturity, and athletic ability. Each player should have a specifically designed improvement plan in virtually every subject being taught. Players also are further divided by position skills and concepts to be mastered.

Parents, Boosters, and Fans

For a program to be successful, the players require support from parents, boosters, and fans. Attention should be given to the kind of information you provide to this group of students to maximize their support, such as educating parents about team rules and player nutrition.

The Team

A frequently overlooked student is the team itself. Every team develops a unique personality. This results from mostly intangible variables that lead to a cohesion of group identity, attitude, and behavior. Depending on the number of available teachers, some programs break down the team into offensive, defensive, and special units and further divide into offensive-and defensive-position units. There is no defined learning progression with clear goals, so this teaching is art, not science, and is the most challenging responsibility for a coach. The measure of a team is found in the components of coordinated movement, player-to-player communication, anticipation of teammate reactions, and understanding of strategic goals.

TEAM-SPORT SUBJECTS

Although the various students in a sport program may vary considerably, the subjects for each sport are clear but perhaps not as well recognized as they should be. The effectiveness of teaching will depend on focused awareness of these subjects in every part of program planning. When considered as a discrete element of the total program, each subject involves different aspects of learning theory and teaching techniques.

Playing Skills

The most obvious subject for any game is the set of athletic skills necessary for success in the sport. Fortunately, time and experience have refined and defined the skill sets into a proven progression from novice to expert. How students learn these skills is less clear, because the teacher is a critical element in recognizing the individual learning style of each pupil. The teacher must also be adept at recognizing the appropriate steps in the learning progression for each skill. Advanced and expert-level teaching will also incorporate self-assessment, transfer of learning to new situations, and strategic comprehension into the skill-development progression.

The Game

Players need to learn the rules of the game, how to play it, and the strategies that are used to win. Every game has an object. The object may be as simple as hide and seek. In field sports, the object is to pass the ball between players to obtain open shots at the goal. In football, the object is for eleven players to work together to either help or stop a single player from advancing the ball toward the goal line. Teaching can progress to more-complex situational concepts relating to score, time, tactics, and use of the playing area. This body of knowledge is sometimes referred to as "football IQ," which is developed in part by rote learning and in part by teaching comprehensive concepts, such as why things are done the way they are.

The Playbook

Every team has a clear plan for the coordinated movement of players during a game. Learning these movements (the playbook) is essential before any player can participate effectively with the team. Again, advanced teaching will incorporate a comprehension of strategic concepts, tactical adjustments, and a language system necessary to communicate the playbook.

Motivation to Learn

Students may need to know how to learn, so some aspects of learning theory, such as attention, memory, and self-assessment, should be early subjects you teach them. Skill development also depends on learning the personal habits, attitudes, and work ethic necessary for growth and success. Teaching these elements requires the coach to create an environment where it is fun to learn and where everything the team does is about learning to become better.

Teamwork

Although learning to work together is an essential subject for success, this learning is an intensively interactive experience for each unique team. It starts with an understanding of the roles for each position and how that position works with the rest of the team. Advanced teaching focuses on communication, mutual action/reaction, and a keen awareness of how each individual team member fulfills his or her role during the game. The mental attitudes for competitive success are infused in everything the team does.

The fundamental subjects for teaching teamwork are detailed in Karlene Sugarman's *Winning the Mental Game* (Burlingame, CA: Step Up Press, 1999), which teaches the mental attitudes that can be addressed and taught in the team's practice sessions and group activities.

The subtle psychological and philosophical aspects of teamwork can be found in Daniel James Brown's *The Boys in the Boat* (New York: Penguin Books, 2014), the best-selling story of the eight-man rowing crew that won a gold medal at the 1936 Berlin Olympic Games. After four years of grueling practice to perfect their rowing technique, the coach and crew were still seeking consistent teamwork. The answer was found by the team's boatbuilder and player confidant, George Pocock. "If you don't like some fellow in the boat, Joe, you have to learn to like him. It has to matter to you whether he wins the race, not just whether you do … Joe, when you really start trusting those other boys, you will feel a power at work within you that is far beyond anything you've ever imagined. Sometimes, you will feel as if you have rowed right off the planet and are rowing among the stars."[4]

Body Awareness and Physical Development

Especially for early-level players, it is important to develop an awareness of how the body moves, functions, and develops. This starts with proper stretching and warm-up, a focus on increasing agility and speed, the building of strength and endurance, and basic biofeedback, such as breathing and relaxation. Advanced programs use strength coaches, nutritionists, and sports psychologists for these subjects.

Game Experience

Practices can be structured to simulate game play by involving as many components of game experience as possible. For example, set drills and run-throughs for specific situations, such as coping with third-down pressure, handling turnovers and bad breaks, creating adrenaline and momentum, and conditioning for the game-time pace of play. However, there is no substitute for taking the field in a game uniform before a crowd and facing the speed and talent of an opponent. It is important to provide game experience to

---

[4] Daniel James Brown, *The Boys in the Boat* (New York: Penguin Books, 2014), 235.

second-and third-team players, not only for each player's personal enjoyment, but also for the overall quality of the team's play when injuries or fatigue require substitution for a first-team player. Look for every opportunity to add depth to the team's game experience. Many programs keep a log of minutes or play reps for every player to organize the process and assure consistent improvement.

Behavior

Player behavior, on and off the field, is an increasing focus in competitive sports. Although changes at the professional level may be driven by marketing and public pressure, amateur team sports have set standards and expectations for their programs. Teaching those standards and properly conveying the players' responsibility to represent teammates and the program are now important subjects in all team sports. Great coaches have always taught that. John Wooden, Hall of Fame coach of the UCLA Bruins basketball dynasty, focused on player behavior as a key component of a successful team. He said, "You cannot attain and maintain physical condition unless you are morally and mentally conditioned. And it is impossible to be in moral condition unless you are spiritually conditioned. I always told my players that our team condition depended on two factors: how hard they worked on the floor during practice and how well they behaved between practices."[5]

Competitive team sports require good behavior on and off the field. Players should be taught the behavior standards expected among teammates and the individual behavior expected of those who want to belong to the team. On-the-field respect for opponents, fair play, and emotional control are lessons that can be taught at any time. Dealing with teammates requires an understanding of brotherhood and sisterhood, mutual support, and loyalty. Explain to players their behavioral responsibilities and help them to appreciate their roles as representatives of the team in the community and as examples for young fans.

---

[5] Hand, *Defensive Coordinator's Football Handbook*, 228.

HOW PLAYERS LEARN

Every Student Is Unique

Effective teaching is a two-party process between a teacher and student(s). The process is not successful if the student does not learn the subject matter. Educational psychology focuses on how students learn, so teachers can present lessons in the manner that has the best chance of success. The key concepts in educational psychology that I discuss here are based on my education and experience as a school psychologist. In addition, these concepts have been updated and supported with research studies in the National Research Council's *How People Learn*.[6] Even with the extensive scientific information available about how people learn, there is no simple formula for a successful teacher-student process. The following insights are provided for coaches to consider in getting to know their players as students of the sport.

New Learning

The art of teaching is controlled by the wide variety of individual differences that each student brings to a new learning experience, particularly the different ways each student takes in information and the different levels of existing knowledge and experience.

Information is received through sensory modalities like vision, hearing, smell, and kinesthesia (awareness of body position and movement). Each student has preferred modes of receiving information. The preference may be genetic, organic (biological), or experiential and is independent of the student's intelligence and motivation. Teaching activities should attempt to address each student's best modalities whenever possible.

In addition, all learning is based on and starts with a student's existing knowledge and experience. This individual student profile includes the following three aspects:

---

[6] National Research Council, *How People Learn*, ed. John D. Bransford, Ann L. Brown, and Rodney R. Cocking (Washington, DC: National Academy Press, 2000).

1. Prior context. If the subject is long division, does the student know multiplication? If the subject is a new offensive formation, has the student first learned the basic player positions and roles?
2. Prior learning experiences. A student's previous learning experiences may have been negative, boring, or unsuccessful. The student may have been taught the wrong information in the past or may have misunderstood or drawn the wrong conclusions from the taught material. For example, a student may believe that running a play is about getting to a final position rather than taking a very specific path to get there. A student new to a sport may assume that all sports are played the same and try to fit all new instructions into that concept. Military shooting instructors typically start every student with the basics to correct and eliminate the bad habits that they may arrive with. Prior learning may have been focused on a different teaching goal—for example, knowledge-based goals with a focus on interactive and questioning teaching methods, rather than performance-based goals (with a focus on skill development with goal attainment).
3. Learning skills. Students may have learned a lot of information in their life but not developed good learning habits. Cultural and family background also directly impact the habits students bring to learning. Successful learning is enhanced when students focus attention, improve concentration, extend memory skills, and foster intellectual curiosity.

An advanced learning skill applicable to sports is inner game theory. W. Timothy Gallwey explains the concept of inner game theory in his book *The Inner Game of Tennis* (New York: Random House, 2008). The theory is that the human nervous system can function much more quickly than the human brain. For example, hitting a tennis serve or baseball is accomplished by nervous system reaction, not conscious direction from the brain, because the conscious mind does not work fast enough. Many motor activities, such as throwing and catching a ball or shooting a basket, are accomplished on a neuromuscular level for the same reason. Being late, on anything from throwing a pass to making a block, is a symptom that there is too much thinking going on. Learning inner game theory can enable players to master new skills simply by internalizing correct examples and repeating the activity until the body gets it right. For example, I learned all the movements for playing second base by watching major-league second basemen play the position. Advanced sports programs teach inner game theory along with similar concepts of visualization and biofeedback.

The individual differences that comprise each student should be considered when forming a student-teacher relationship. Advanced teaching can include formative assessment of what knowledge each student brings to the lesson. This is accomplished by documenting a baseline level of skill development; reviewing foundational information to correct errors, bad habits, and misconceptions; and instructing the student in learning skills.

Learning and Retention

The essence of learning is the ability to add information to one's existing knowledge base and retain the information received. We have all known people who do not seem to learn from experience or who walk out of a class and cannot recall anything that was discussed. Retaining new information involves context and memory.

Developing context.[7]

The components of an individual's knowledge base influence how that person perceives and organizes new information. This context can be viewed as a personal filing system. If you see a seven-digit number like 735-9308, you may automatically assume it is a phone number. That may not be a correct assumption, but that is the context in which you will receive and file the information.

When you teach an athletic skill, you should do so in context. For

---

[7] National Research Council, "How Children Learn," chap. 4 in *How People Learn*.

example, you should teach it as a step in personal development, as part of a play, or as part of the role for the position being taught. A playbook should be taught in the context of the formations, strategies, and style of play the team uses. Advanced concepts or actions also have a more advanced context, such as the correct tactical response to a specific movement by an opponent player. Developmental skills like conditioning can be presented in the context of body awareness and goals to be attained. Developmental progressions like skiing work well in the context of key principles that remain constant throughout the progression: square shoulders, knee movement, and edge awareness.

Retaining knowledge.

Using context is one technique for helping students organize and retain knowledge. Understanding memory—how people retain and retrieve information—can enhance learning. Research into the physiology and functioning of our brains supports a vast base of experimental learning theory that identifies focused awareness, emotion, association, and repetition as effective techniques to retain information.[8]

- *Focused awareness.* Our bodies are bombarded by countless impulses every second, but we can perceive only a small amount of the information at any one time. For example, certain sound frequencies and light wavelengths do not register on our sensory receptors. Dogs hear things we can't, and antelope see us long before we see them. We know infrared light waves exist, but we cannot see them. *Perception* is the impulses we can receive. Of the perceptible information available to us, we can focus our attention on only a very small percentage. For example, we usually ignore traffic noise unless we hear a siren or a crash. American Indians and some military personnel can smell smoke and

---

[8] National Research Council, "How Children Learn," chap. 4 in *How People Learn.*

food over long distances, while most of us ignore many of the odors in our world.

We only remember those images on which we intentionally focus our attention, so recognizing and controlling attention is a key component of learning. Short attention spans can result in disorganized behavior and ineffective learning. Better focus is developed by generating interest in the subject of one's focus. Having a purpose for the focus can also help people maintain interest in a subject. Attention spans can be increased by practice and by self-instruction. For example, people can say to themselves, "I know this lecture is boring, but I will continue to focus and try to find some way to make it interest me." Focused attention is a critical element of teaching and is why so much of teaching involves maintaining the students' interest.

- *Emotion.* I believe that we only remember information that is attached to an emotion. This theory may explain why we often have clear memories of certain songs that are only meaningful because of how we felt at the time we heard them. Emotion can also have a negative impact on learning and memory. Worry, fear, or depression can distract attention and divert interest. Students can be taught to control their emotions in many situations, including learning. Students can also be taught to combine focused attention with emotional control to achieve a sense of peace or calm. Principles of Zen consciousness are reflected in hobbies like fly-fishing and skiing and in those times when an athlete is in the zone. The role of emotion in learning emphasizes the importance of atmosphere in a learning environment.
- *Association.* Association is a technique to improve memory, especially the ability to recall information. Association involves connecting discrete pieces of information so that recalling one piece leads to the next. For example, a stranger's name can be remembered by associating it with the stranger's facial features, appearance, or job. Dean Vaughn presents

a comprehensive review of these techniques in *How to Remember Anything.*

- *Repetition.* Repeating information and activities improves memory. Physiological research suggests that repetition develops new synapses in the nervous system, like new wiring in your computer memory.[9] Note that repetition must involve all the components of memory, so simply going through the motions will not be effective or create new synapses.

FIVE TEACHING TECHNIQUES FOR COACHES

All teaching techniques start with and focus on the student and require the use of skills appropriate for the student and subject matter of each learning activity.

Understand Developmental Sequence

Whether the subject being taught is a skill, the game, the playbook, the team, or behavioral attitudes, understanding the progression of learning for the subject is essential to presenting information in an organized way. For example, in mathematics, addition is taught before subtraction, and in sports skills, body position is taught before movement. This is called a *developmental sequence* and is reflected in terms like *fundamentals*, the *basics*, and the *next level*. The developmental sequence is critical to a student's ability to transfer knowledge to new situations, to develop a correct context for each lesson, to comprehend the principles that underlie the learning, and to perform effective self-assessment.

Every developmental sequence has a micro and a macro component. The detailed view of a skill like skiing includes foot, knee, hip, arm, and head position as well as weight transfer. The big picture of the developmental sequence begins with putting the tips of the skis together and bending the knees to make a snowplow

---

[9] National Research Council, "Mind and Brain," chap. 5 in *How People Learn.*

turn. That position then changes to lifting the uphill ski and putting it beside the downhill ski to make a step turn. Finally, the skier keeps the skis together and parallel, turning one knee to shift weight to the inside edge of a ski to make a parallel turn. The body positions change as the student advances through each stage of development. Note the tremendous number of detailed changes that occur and the fact that the resulting action looks totally different from the starting point.

Before a student can advance along a developmental sequence, you must know where the student is in his or her development, so first determine the student's current subject knowledge. If the subject is a skill, close observation can reveal the next step to teach. For example, in catching a ball, the student may not be positioning his or her palms correctly to receive the ball or may not be looking the ball into the hands or may not be moving the ball to the next position for required action. This observation to determine where a student is in the developmental sequence is a constant process that separates a good teacher from an ineffective one.

Communicate Information Effectively

Because learning occurs through multiple modalities of vision, hearing, attention, and kinetics, an effective teacher should master all methods of communicating information.

- Visual presentations should include attention-getting graphics, clear organization (like PowerPoint), and video or real-time demonstrations. For skills, it is helpful to show the student what correct execution looks like. If you follow inner game theory, do not have students watch bad examples of anything.
- Verbal presentations should be well delivered, concise, interesting, persuasive, and interactive. One way to make them interactive is to invite questions and feedback.
- Sports are movement oriented, so teaching should be as well. While skill subjects are obviously taught using movement, other subjects can also incorporate movement. For example, you can walk or run through the playbook,

and teamwork can involve coordinated exercise and group movement, the trading of positions, and reactive responses to teammate movement. Slow motion is effective in developing comprehension of strategy concepts, tactical applications, and reaction to opponent movement. Body awareness and feedback is an essential part of conditioning and skill performance.

Maintain Pupil Motivation

You can maintain your students' motivation to learn with a variety of techniques. Sustained interest results from the learning atmosphere. The pace of learning is a function of balancing challenge and success. If the lessons are learning oriented, the motivation is for more information; if performance oriented, the motivation is to eliminate mistakes and improve competence. Most important is providing positive reinforcement, ranging from teacher attention or praise to teammate recognition, advancement on a depth chart, and attainment of team goals. Use of the Socratic method involves asking questions and having the students discover the answers for themselves. For example, asking why a play is designed the way it is can lead students to a better understanding of strategic design for both offensive and defensive players. Using players to teach each other builds teamwork and requires the players to develop a deep enough understanding of the subject that they can teach it to others.

Focused attention is necessary for effective learning, so teaching activities should be designed to focus attention through verbal cues like calling out a name or command, changing volume and pace, and asking questions. Shifting to and from visual presentations and demonstrations also helps maintain attention.

Generalized attention should be addressed to reduce distractions caused by personal problems, off-field pursuits, off-task behavior, and emotional blocking resulting from frustration and mistakes. For example, a sign visible when leaving the locker room, ritual behaviors before entering the practice area, group activities at the start of practice, on-field discipline, and instruction on emotional control are all effective techniques in maintaining everyone's attention on the business at hand.

Use Assessment

Assessment of student learning is a key component of teaching. Effective assessment is more than periodic testing and review. It is an interactive, integrated element of every teaching activity that begins with finding the baseline levels of functioning and comprehension for the subject being taught. The process can continue through more-advanced comprehension of tactical concepts, such as using the correct technique in a specific situation. Postperformance assessment is a critical learning opportunity.

Assessment focuses on both the student and the teacher. Students can self-assess their performance through techniques as simple as proofing the answer to a math problem, asking questions to confirm understanding, watching video of past performance, or watching instructive examples. Teachers can assess their effectiveness in each lesson and the success of various teaching techniques. The total coach will assess every aspect of his or her program.

Understanding the way knowledge is transferred to new subjects and learning experiences is part of the assessment process. Testing whether a student has memorized information does not reveal anything about whether the student can use that information in future learning. For example, a player can memorize a play from the playbook but will not be able to run the play from a new formation unless he or she has also learned the design of the play. Teaching a play from a new formation should start with an assessment of whether the student understands the play design goals that do not change. Transfer can also be enhanced by having players learn new positions or switch responsibilities between offense and defense.

Avoid Degradation in Learning

Degradation is the natural tendency to conserve energy, take the easy way, and cut corners. It reflects a regression of learned behavior or information. Good examples of cutting corners are the pass receiver who is coached to run a sharp, square-out pattern but regresses to a lazy, banana-shaped curve and the player who stops moving his or her feet before getting to the correct position. Degradation of performance is also reflected in fatigue, so increasing endurance improves performance. Again, just going through the motions without focus and correction will not be effective. This is a situation that requires the coach to maintain focused attention on the activity. There was an entire season when I observed that my team's defensive ends would forget to jam inside receivers in goal line defense practice; it cannot be assumed that practice alone will fix the problem. Avoiding degradation should be a coach's primary focus on run-throughs the day before a game.

TEACHING FOR ENTRY-LEVEL PROGRAMS

Most advanced-level programs screen their talent and may not spend much effort in trying to develop raw talent. By contrast, entry-level programs receive players with a mix of talent and sports experience, and, in many cases, these players may even lack the physical maturity necessary to safely engage in the sport at full competitive levels. These players may have little or no knowledge of what it is like to play the game and no idea whether they will like it. The differences are evident in two fundamental aspects of competitive team sports: physical conditioning and physical contact, which both involve pain. Accepting these aspects of any sport is a *learned* decision. Therefore, a primary focus of entry-level activities is teaching participants what is necessary for success and doing it in small, measured steps. For example, teach running and agility before engaging in wind sprints, and teach players how to fall and move on the ground before adding player-to-player contact. Teach players that there is a difference between tired and exhausted and between sore muscles and torn muscles before expecting them to push their personal limits.

The goals for entry-level sports should be squarely centered on the quality of the experience provided to *every* participant. Even if a player decides that he or she does not have the physical or mental qualities to succeed in the sport, that decision belongs to the player, not the prejudgments and expectations of the coach. The decision should be based on a fair chance to learn and experience the sport. Providing a quality experience requires a coach to look at the sport with a different point of view that focuses on teaching, practice, and competition as well as on the activities that comprise the essence of the sport. It is also important to keep in mind that your sport may be the only safe haven a child has from negative school or family environments. The following activities illustrate some ways to provide fun, satisfaction, and a true team experience while developing a very competitive team.

Know the Ball

Whatever it is called and whatever its shape, team sports are played with a central object (ball) and a set of rules for how the ball is handled. The first thing new players should learn is how to handle the ball, how it moves, and how to possess it. Observing people of any age handle a ball demonstrates the satisfaction in attempting the diving catches and pinpoint passes seen on TV. Acquire as many extra balls as possible and have players hold them while standing around, while running, and while completing some warm-up activities. Teach handoffs and catches, how to recover loose balls, and how to take possession away from opponents. Every player should have these experiences, not only for their own sake but also to allow the coach full opportunity to assess the talent. For example, a big, slow lineman may have great hands for catching passes or great play recognition, and an undersized defensive back may have great reaction to the ball.

Teach the Positions

Teamwork begins when every player knows his or her job and everyone else's. Most new players do not understand that every offensive player has some blocking responsibilities and that every defensive position can have an area to defend. For every new play that is taught, teach the job of every position. Remember, the mantra of championship teams is often "Do your job."

Be a Team

Rotate leaders, on and off the field, and visit upper-level competition. Everyone should get a team symbol—a T-shirt, a ball, a team picture, or something that shows they worked for the team.

Teach Competition

Competition in team sports—and life—can no longer be taken for granted. Competition is a zero-sum game; for every winner there is a loser. Because losing is a difficult and often painful experience, some people attempt to make all of life and especially youth sports into win-win experiences. The simple solution of avoiding competitive sports or turning all competitive sports into noncompetitive group activities ignores the real issue. The reward and satisfaction in all competition is not in winning; it comes from focusing effort, overcoming the risk of failure, and achieving both personal and team goals. That is why defeating an obviously inferior opponent offers little satisfaction. Unfortunately, many coaches in entry-level competitive sports overlook the true values of competition and focus only on winning. Because most entry-level athletes have not learned or experienced the work, pain, and disappointment necessary to enjoy the rewards of competition, a win-at-all-costs coaching approach leaves them with a negative, unsatisfactory experience. The answer is to adjust the coaching goals and the sport experience to set the foundation for individual growth, self-confidence, and satisfaction. Providing the experiences discussed herein for young players may result in more-competitive teams than can be achieved by focusing on individual talent and competition for playing time, as is common in advanced-level programs.

1. I suggest the following goals for entry-level coaches: Keep it simple. Use clear, easy-to-remember terminology. Run straight ahead with safe handoffs and simple timing. Use basic rules for blocking, pass routes, and coverages. Limit the number of formations and base defenses.
2. Focus on the fundamentals of the game. Remember that this may be a player's first experience with the sport. (I remember

how grateful I was when an older player showed me how to put on the pads.) Limit hitting to padded dummies and sleds. In shooting, it is easy to develop a flinch if the gun is too big. The same can happen with full-speed contact before a player has learned the correct positions and the feel of contact. Teach every detail that experienced players take for granted, from where to line up to stopping on the whistle.

3. Use the best players on both offense and defense. Everybody used to do it that way, and many sports still do. Find the aggressive players, and place them in the key positions. Then plan substitutions from the starting lineup.

4. Create advantages with strategy. In entry-level programs every team has roughly the same talent pool, so most success results from coaching. Focus the strength of offensive formations, and then attack weaknesses and mistakes in defensive alignment and coverage. Plan for two-minute and come-from-behind situations. Use simple blitzes, goal line defenses, and slants to strength. Create surprises by using a few unusual formations like unbalanced lines and stacked running backs for short yardage. Install the opportunity to snap the ball on the first sound or on a tap from the quarterback. Prepare for and practice special situations like short yardage, red zone, and trick plays.

CHAPTER 3
YOUR SPORTS PROGRAM

IF THE COACH DOES NOT KNOW WHAT
IS HAPPENING, WHO DOES?

I n managing a law firm with my partner for twenty-two years and in serving as a board chairman of the Ohio League Against Child Abuse and later the Jackson/Teton County Joint Powers Recycling Board, I learned that every program and organization requires management of its component parts. Successful coaches must assume the duties of a manager. Whatever the level of the program under a coach's charge, even if it is part of a larger program, successful management begins with an understanding of the elements that are included in that program. This understanding is necessary because a coach is responsible for everything that happens within the program, whether he or she knows about what is happening or not. Program management is also the place to address current concerns in team sports, such as player safety, sportsmanship and ethical behavior, qualifications and training for program personnel, and the quality of the experience provided to players.

KNOW YOUR PROGRAM

The skills and leadership traits of a total coach are not reserved for the locker room and practice field. They are required in every aspect of the program. The team is the central element of a sports program, and every other element in the program should be coordinated to support the team and achieve the coach's vision of the program. The personnel of the program—the coaches, staff, and volunteers—require leadership, training, and the tools to do their jobs. Including parents, boosters, and, ideally, former players in the program can add invaluable support for the team and the program. The more integrally these people are involved in the program activities, the stronger their contributions and loyalty.

Facilities. An element of the program that can easily be overlooked or taken for granted is the space, equipment, and supplies necessary for efficient operations. Even at the youth-league level, the team needs uniforms, training supplies, hydration, nutrition, and possible transportation. I have seen teams arrive for games only to find that the playing area was not available or not prepared or that equipment had been forgotten or not operable. The facilities are also an important consideration for player safety.

Resources. Operating any program requires equipment, uniforms, athletic training supplies, facilities, and other supplies. League rules and academic regulations may dictate the permissible financial sources of these program components in the interest of fair competition. Within these rules, resources may be available from the program budget, parents, fan support, and community sponsors. You should prepare an annual plan to acquire, replace, and maintain the program resources.

Rules. Every program must be operated within the rules. These extend beyond the rules of the game to league rules, possible academic requirements, and medical regulations, including HIPAA medical privacy. It is the coach's responsibility to know the rules and to see that they are enforced. Not only is this the right approach, but the consequences of breaking the rules can damage the coach's reputation and the program's integrity. As a board member of many nonprofit organizations, I reviewed board decisions with a focus on the program's mission statement and on the possible damage that a wrong decision would do to the program's reputation and integrity. Before breaking a rule, realize that you are teaching your players that they cannot win by playing within the rules.

Security. Perhaps the most neglected element of program administration is security. In today's environment, security issues reach every aspect of the program. Security begins with control of access to all program areas, starting with player areas such as locker rooms and sidelines/benches. It extends to securing program equipment from theft or vandalism. And finally, it covers securing all program information that should remain confidential, such as player and personnel files, playbooks, and practice sessions. Observe the elaborate steps coaches take to code and conceal game-time communications.

CONTROL YOUR PROGRAM

Control is achieved through effective management, which requires skills in communication, organizational structure, personnel training, planning, and data collection.

Communication within the program should be appropriate to its purpose. For example, it may be fine to yell out your car window to ask the groundskeeper whether the sprinklers are turned off at the game field, but bookings for officials and transportation should be confirmed in writing. Personnel matters should be handled with respect and confidence. People within the program should be communicating regularly and appropriately with each other. It is helpful to develop a communication system within the program to readily reach staff, parents, and players.

Personal communication skills are essential to teaching and to sharing your goals and vision for the program. A coach's personal communication style is a direct reflection of the coach's character. The following principles should shape your personal communication style:

1. Your word is your bond. Don't make a promise you do not intend to keep.
2. Think first. You can't take what you say back.
3. Don't say anything about someone that you can't say to their face.
4. Vulgarity is not strength and is disrespectful to the listener.
5. Use clear standards and expectations rather than orders and demands.

Master the following communication techniques that are essential in interpersonal communication: listen, confirm, recognize, and provide context. *Communicating Effectively* by Saundra Hybels and Richard L. Weaver II is a textbook introduction to the art of personal communication and public speaking.

Program organization is necessary to get things done as planned, on schedule and on time. All activities should mutually support the program goals. Essential resources should be procured, maintained, and used efficiently. Everyone in the program should be accountable to someone for doing his or her job. A training program should be in place so everyone knows how to do his or her job competently. Job performance should be regularly assessed, with understood consequences and reinforcement.

Separate program systems can be established for any activities requiring regulatory compliance, such as player safety, team medical support and coordination, league rules, academic requirements and eligibility, and confidentiality of private information.

Systems should be established for organizing and filing program records. If the coach is a chronic throw-it-in-a-drawer or can't-find-it type, then someone should be delegated to manage the records. Program resources should also include technology for communication and information management, along with the personnel to use it.

Organizational planning techniques are now well recognized, and both written materials and personal facilitators are available to teach or guide the planning process. A key element of leadership is setting a direction for a program. Setting goals for an organization starts with an understanding of the organization's mission and a vision of what the organization should look like three or five years in the future. You can then make a plan of how the organization can achieve its vision and decide on annual and long-term goals to accomplish each element of the plan. This type of comprehensive planning should address all the components of the program, from facilities to the team.

The structure of an organization reflects the leadership style and vision statement of the leader. The structure should be a conscious decision and not left to chance or individual personalities. It is the pathway through which a coach exercises control over every aspect of the program. There are two general types of pathways, vertical and horizontal. Each has strengths and weaknesses that should be considered relative to the program plans and the coach's personality.

In vertical organization, decisions are made at the top for everything that happens in the program. There are clear lines of communication, and the personal relationships tend to be of a formal superior-subordinate type. This structure is focused on maintaining a coach's control over everything that happens in the program. The weakness of a vertical structure is that it slows decision-making while a question makes its way to the top or while a subordinate looks for the answer by consulting established policies. Little initiative or spontaneity is left to subordinate personnel.

Horizontal structure diffuses control across separate aspects of the program, each with its own manager. For example, a team sport may have an offensive coordinator, a defensive coordinator, an equipment and training manager, and an administrator. Each department is comprised of its own divisions, such as line coach, quarterback coach, and receivers coach. The manager of each division makes decisions in accord with the goals and strategies set by the head coach. Communication can be informal both vertically and between managers because of the teamwork involved in reaching program goals.

ASSUME RESPONSIBILITY

Coaches are given awesome responsibilities. Parents trust coaches with the safety and well-being of their children, *in loco parentis*. Parents also trust coaches to provide success in many aspects of their child's personal development. Competitive organizations expect well-run, successful programs. Finally, everything that happens in a program reflects on the character of the person in charge.

PLAYER SAFETY

The responsibility for player safety is entrusted to a coach by parents, but it also arises from the coach's personal ethical obligation to place player safety above personal and team goals, even if the parents do not. The coach's responsibility is especially critical when dealing with younger players who do not have the physical development to perform some skills required in the sport and who have not learned how to protect themselves from the injury risks inherent in the sport. Player safety is achieved by creating a safe environment to prevent injuries and providing the proper resources and procedures to treat injuries when they occur.

A Safe Environment

Creating a safe environment is a management role involving every aspect of the program. Practice and play areas should have unobstructed boundaries, protection from obstacles, safe equipment, and clearly assigned maneuvering areas. Player equipment should meet applicable safety standards and be regularly inspected and maintained. Safety programs such as Heads Up[10] and concussion protocols are examples of safety considerations in designing practice activities and lessons. Review each planned drill for safety and age-appropriate physical demands. Safe transportation is essential and carries added legal duties and liabilities that should not be dealt with casually. All player areas should also be sanitary and protected from communicable infections.

Medical and Health Services

Sports programs require a physician's opinion that each player is fit to play. However, the role of the medical community in team sports should not be limited to preseason checkups and the treatment of injuries after they occur. Health-critical situations, such as on-field injuries and chronic conditions like asthma and diabetes, require immediate or active medical intervention.

Medical services are a component of program administration. If not provided by the sponsoring organization, on-field medical support can be obtained using community volunteers. Note that an

---

[10] Heads Up is a safety-instruction program that has served over seven thousand youth and high school programs. For more information, see https://www.usafootball.com/development-training/certification, accessed October 26, 2017.

untrained coach should never make the decision whether to move someone with a possible spinal cord injury. Protocols and procedures should be established for the program to provide coordination with medical treatment directives and precautions. First aid training for program staff can also be obtained, and advanced seminars are available to coaches. A serious injury or condition file should be maintained for any such situation that arises.

Creating a Training Program

Advanced competitive programs include certified sports training support. If such support is not provided, the coach can obtain and train volunteers or students to provide athletic training services. Necessary supplies and services should be identified. These include everything from on-field hydration to preventative taping and whirlpool programs. You can determine the priorities for your program by reviewing the national certification programs for athletic trainers.

A Safe Experience for Players

Consider injury prevention when selecting practice drills and practice activities. Do not engage in team movement activities without pads, mouthpieces, and headgear. Assure adequate space for each activity, free from equipment and other activities. Adjust practice activities for adverse weather conditions or poor field conditions.

Limit hitting to padded dummies and sleds. Stand-alone dummies and large blocking pads are great teaching aids that should be used to reduce the risk of injuries in practice.

Using dummies offers subtle advantages for new players that extend beyond the obvious features of the dummies standing still and not hitting back. For example, by using dummies, the correct positions for movements from blocking to open-field footwork can be taught at full speed without player-to-player contact. Using multiple dummies can enhance coordinated movement drills by simulating offensive and defensive alignments. For example, three dummies can define the A and B line gaps for lead blockers or defenders while providing a clear framework for teaching numerous individual offensive and defensive skills. Adding a second-level dummy can provide a ball carrier for defenders or a linebacker for blockers. Blocking pads also provide more reps in the available time, permitting both offensive and defensive players to experience the drill. It is easy to move progressively from one drill to another with a simple reset of the dummies.

CHAPTER 4
THINK LIKE A STRATEGIST

SEE EVERYTHING IN LIFE IN TERMS OF YOUR GOALS.

A s early as the fourth century BC, Sun Tzu's *The Art of War* was being discussed in the context of philosophies propounded by Confucius, Socrates, and the Jewish Torah. *The Art of War* is an approach to life that uses strategic thinking to overcome nonnegotiable obstacles in achieving personal goals.[11] Thinking strategically is a scientific process based on mathematical probabilities, as in card playing, dice games, and baseball statistics, or in the analysis of complex movements and objectives. Strategic thinking also requires a personal expression of courage and imagination in planning the strategic systems and tactical devices to achieve a desired goal.

Because strategic thinking is a component of any game, from solitaire to team sports, it is essential that a coach understand the principles of strategic thinking and how to apply those principles in planning the team's competitive performance. Being an effective strategist is the heart of coaching and the source of great personal satisfaction. In the words from *The A-Team* TV show, "I love it when a plan comes together." The mental and creative aspects of strategy are a complement to the athletic parts of a game. The first step in being an effective strategist is to learn to look at every situation from a strategic point of view. The examples throughout this chapter are intended to illustrate both the concepts being discussed as well as the types of available information that can assist in making strategic decisions.

---

[11] Sun Tzu, *The Art of Strategy: A New Translation of Sun Tzu's Classic, "The Art of War,"* trans. R. L. Wing (New York: Doubleday, 1988).

The role of strategic thinking and its importance in team sports is too often ignored as coaches jump ahead to the popular systems seen on TV or the newest software for designing a playbook. None of those resources will work if the coach does not understand the strategic and tactical components that underlie each system and play.

Program strategy is developed with very general but difficult decisions. It then proceeds through more-detailed levels to the specific tactics for specific opponents (and in advanced programs, to specific opponent players). The strategy development process should be followed for offensive, defensive, and special situations.

Strategy is employed through selected tactics. For example, in a team sport, the chosen strategy may be to use speed to achieve offensive goals. Possible tactics could involve spreading the playing area to gain space to outmaneuver defenders; outflanking defenders; using quick, slashing moves through the defense; and moving the point of attack to unexpected areas. Unfortunately, most of what we see of sports strategy is the execution played out game by game through a season, but the strategies for offense and defense seen on game day are planned and practiced before the season begins.

SELECT STRATEGIC SYSTEMS

Selecting new strategies or reviewing established ones requires consideration of the operational variables that are necessary to execute the chosen strategy.

Execution by the Coaching Staff

The coaching staff should be familiar with and understand executing the system in all aspects. This includes understanding the principles relating to field position, time clock, and game adjustments. If the available staff does not have the sophistication or experience to learn the system, they will not be able to teach, communicate, or practice effectively.

Maintaining the Desired Risk Level

Understanding risk is an element of strategic thinking. For example, if controlling time of possession is a strategy, then low-risk, high-success plays generate first downs and continued possession. That strategic concept is referred to as *staying ahead of the [first-down] chains*. Today's triple-option run by Navy or the short passing of some spread offenses are examples of this strategic system.

Risk can be viewed as the possibility of an adverse consequence from a chosen action. The consequence may be failure, a minor setback, or a major loss of momentum, and the likelihood of a bad result may be high or low. To fully understand risk, it is necessary to consider the possible rewards of the chosen action. These rewards may similarly be great or small and likely or unlikely. Managing risk is the process of evaluating the good and bad consequences against the possibility of their occurrence. For example, throwing a pass has a risk that the ball will be dropped or, worse, intercepted. These risks are very low for a short, five-yard pass but much higher for a longer, thirty-yard pass.

While the results of a chosen action are determined by any number of uncontrolled, random variables, there are many variable influences that can be controlled, calculated, or eliminated. Some controllable variables can be identified by commonsense analysis. For example, throwing a wet ball in the rain increases the chance it will be dropped, and high wind increases the chance it will be intercepted. Throwing a pass against an opponent's best defender will have a greater chance of adverse consequences than throwing against a substitute or slower defender. The same is true for running the ball when all defenders expect a run.

Some variables can be controlled by practice. Practicing any skill can improve execution and the likelihood of success. Practicing passes or free throws reduces the number of misses, as does learning and using the proper technique. The more complicated the technique or maneuver, the more variables that can go wrong. For example, a good dive play into the line requires a simple handoff and two good blocks in the B gap, while a reverse or screen pass requires execution by all eleven offensive players over a longer period of time.

There are many variables that can be finely calculated from

reliable historic information. Baseball may provide the best example of using performance statistics to choose actions with the highest chance of success, although other advanced-level team sports are not far behind. Every player can be graded by the team (and by opponents) on such things as success rate against every type of maneuver and technique. The effectiveness of plays or defenses are evaluated against down and distance and against field position. The more information that is reviewed, the more possible it is to calculate the chances of success. For example, if an opponent's defense does not allow runs of more than five yards on third down, the chance of gaining eight yards on third down is much better with a play-action pass than with a run play.

After analysis and consideration, every action still contains an uncontrollable risk of failure or adverse consequences. Risk management cannot control all variables or eliminate failure, no matter how safe the planned action. If one is very, very careful, nothing bad *or good* will ever happen.

It is the coach who must find the rewards. The coach must manage the risks that can be controlled while having the courage to face those that can't.

Player Knowledge and Experience

The more complex the chosen system, the more it is dependent on player practice and experience. If a program has high player turnover, then a system with complicated communication, multiple reads and adjustments, or closely coordinated team action cannot be effectively executed within the practice time available. For advanced programs with players moving from elementary to junior and then varsity teams, the system should be taught and practiced at an early, simplified level to create a pipeline of players with the skill development and experience to execute the program systems.

Athletic Skill Requirements

The ability to perform athletic skills is dependent on a combination of natural talent and developmental practice. The athletic skills required to execute the chosen system can vary widely. A clear example is found in the possible strategies for passing offenses and defenses. Throwing, catching, and defending passes one-on-one requires high levels of natural talent and extensive practice time. Passing game strategies should be designed to fit the player skills available.

A critical skill requirement in executing any strategy is physical strength. Every program should have a strength-and-conditioning component, whether in the off-season or during practice. The design and supervision of these activities requires specialized knowledge in player safety and maturational level. The nutritional component may best be achieved by enlisting parental support.

The Competitive Environment

The expected competition for a coming campaign can be a determining factor in designing strategic systems. Using speed is not a strategic advantage if the expected competition has equal or greater speed. If most opponents rely on power-run offenses, then a 3–4 base defense with zone pass coverages will have difficulty in stopping the runs. Similarly, if the competition uses spread offensive systems but does not have the skilled players to operate effectively, then a pressure defensive strategy may create mistakes and turnovers. A more advanced example is competition that rarely uses misdirection, counterplays, or reverses. A defensive system relying on pursuit will be more successful than one based on field balance and complex reads.

To implement a team's strategic systems, the coach should develop a playbook for teaching and operating the system and for practicing correct execution of the system, and the coach should also make use of a game plan to adjust the system to fit a specific opponent's strategic systems and the shifting flow of a game.

DESIGN STRATEGIC SYSTEMS

Strategy in team sports starts with choosing the offensive and defensive system to be used by the team. A system is the combination of the deployment of players and the plans for strategic movement of players. For most sports with relatively continuous play, like soccer and basketball, the system is described as a style of play, such as ball-control offense or sliding-zone defense. In a static, play-by-play game like football, the system is referred to as base formations and type of individual plays.

The offensive and defensive systems used today reflect a wide range of strategies, which offer a general package of strategic objectives like pressure defense or fast-break offense. The systems are implemented through player deployment (think formation or movement patterns, such as spread formations and zone defenses). The deployment is then organized through a series of offensive or defensive plays to achieve the strategic objectives, such as flanking and slashing moves to take advantage of speed. Designing a winning strategy requires the selection of systems based on an understanding of the strengths and weaknesses of each system.

A good place to start is Leo Hand's *Defensive Coordinator's Football Handbook*. Chapter 1 provides a must-read explanation of every significant offensive system that has been developed since the early 1900s. Chapter 2 details a system for quickly identifying offensive formations, and chapter 3 details defensive numbering and lettering systems, with the available complexity to operate professional-level defenses. Chapter 16 offers terminology for multiple defensive stunts and adjustments.

Whatever the sport, the coach can choose to arrange players relative to the rules of play, each other, and the area of play. The deployment used should be chosen to execute the strategic plan. If speed is part of the strategy, then the coach should select deployments with greater maneuvering area. If long passes are planned, then the coach must deploy pass receivers into open passing lanes. Defensive deployments also conform to strategic objectives involving pressure, strengths, and play area—that is, flanks.

Strategic deployments common to team sports all involve a balancing of advantages and disadvantages relative to the level of risk involved. Every strategy has inherent risks of failure to counterbalance the desired strategic objective. Defensive pressure risks major breakdowns. Fast pace could limit offensive possession time. Strength sacrifices speed. Certain pass methods are safer than others, and reliance on reacting to teammate and opponent movement increases the chance of mistakes.

The following discussion of considerations in designing a personal strategic system focuses on football because football deployments are extremely complex due to the number of players involved, the size of the play area, and both offensive and defensive innovations that have evolved in the static, play-by-play nature of the game. Whatever the team sport, coaches can apply the principles of strategic design, selection of tactics, identification of the player skills necessary for effective execution, and development of a language system to their program.

Offensive System Overview

Regardless of the almost infinite number of possible offensive formations that can be deployed, a base formation should be selected to facilitate planning, teaching, communicating, and practicing the system chosen. It does little good to have one hundred plays in the playbook if the team only knows how to deploy and properly execute a few of them. Offensive formations have been developed to implement specific strategies. They each have varying risk levels and critical requirements for effective execution.

The original single-wing and T formations developed before rules were changed to expand the use of the forward pass. These systems, with variations like the power I, veer option, and double wing remain primary run formations because eligible pass receivers are all inside the formation, not separated by more than a few yards from the core group of players.

The pro formation, with a flanker and split end outside the formation, places two pass receivers on the flanks of the defense and gives the tight end more available pass routes. Putting a wingback or slotback on the weak side of the formation (opposite the tight end) results in four quick receivers on the flanks of the defense. The type of available run plays from these formations has increased with the I, split, and pistol backfields. If the available talent can execute a downfield passing attack, the pro formation offers a solid choice for a balanced run-pass system.

Spread formations, sometimes with all eligible receivers on the flanks of the formation, have developed to provide a wide-open passing offense. The number of possible receiver deployments stretches the imagination. Playing out on the flanks, two or three receiver combinations can exploit quick passes, overloads, and crosses into the middle of the field. These systems require advanced skills in passing, route recognition, pass blocking, and reading the defense, both before and after the snap. Running plays from these formations also require specialized blocking and play design.

Defensive System Overview

Defensive systems are all based on three levels: line, linebackers, and safeties. The balance between run defense and pass defense is determined primarily by the number of players at each level. Deployment of defenders also requires a balance of strength on the flanks and in the middle. Size and speed of defenders also varies from large and heavy to light and fast. Defenses are now focused on the eight gaps that are possible along the offensive line of scrimmage and the number of quick pass receivers (outside of the formation) to be covered.

Two critical decisions to begin the design of a defensive strategy are whether to focus on stopping the run or the pass and whether to use a pressure attack or a read-and-react style. Run defense is achieved first by deploying more defenders inside the offensive formation than the offense. Called the *box*, this area typically contains linemen and linebackers. A basic offensive formation can contain seven players on the line of scrimmage within the box. Therefore, a basic run defense will have seven players in the box, usually deployed as linemen and linebackers in formations called 5–2, 4–3, or 3–4. This deployment leaves four pass defenders outside the box, either two safeties and two outside linebackers or three safeties and one linebacker. A spread offensive formation can deploy up to five outside pass receivers (a formation called *empty backfield*). Therefore, a basic pass defense will place six defenders in the box and five pass defenders outside. In addition to the basic run-pass defensive deployments, run defenses are stronger with bigger, hence slower players in the box, while pass defenses are enhanced by faster, more-mobile defenders at all three levels. Some of this shift has been achieved by using only three linemen in the box (3–4) instead of the now outdated 5–2 deployment. For controlling gaps and simplicity of player responsibility, the 5–2 is still a solid choice for entry-level programs.

The second defensive decision involves the level of risk found in two general defensive strategies.

Pressure defenses seek to penetrate the offensive backfield and disrupt plays, cause turnovers, and inflict negative gains. Talent being equal, this style requires a loaded box to outnumber offensive blockers. The result is fewer pass defenders and safeties, which usually dictates one-on-one coverage of pass receivers and fewer second-level run defenders, meaning higher risk.

Reactive defenses focus on controlling the gaps and shifting to the point of attack. These objectives are achieved by "reading" the play, which is a system of specific, planned defensive-player reactions to specific movements of specific offensive players. For example, if the player on the end of the offensive line steps inside, the defender opposite will cross the line and see if the nearest back is moving toward or away from the flank; if the offensive end steps outside, the defender will fight hard to the outside to protect the flank of the defense. When executed effectively, a reactive defense is analogous to an amoeba absorbing and swallowing up its prey. This bend-but-don't-break philosophy focuses on preventing big plays, but the risk is giving up too many easy small plays when reacting to quick-developing plays or dealing with formations or plays that concentrate blockers at the point of attack.

Within the two basic defensive philosophies, tactics begin with the alignment of linemen relative to specific gaps on the line. Advanced programs address up to fifteen possible alignments across the eight-gap line of scrimmage. Linebackers are deployed to achieve gap control, penetration, flank protection, and pass defense. Safeties and outside linebackers can have both run-defense and pass-defense responsibilities, which are generally dictated by whether they are deployed in a specified defensive zone or deployed to cover a specific offensive receiver.

Whether evaluating an existing system or designing a new one, cohesion is a guiding principal. The package of styles, formations, and plays should be consistent with the strategies that underlie the system. For example, if speed is a strategic element, then tight formations and slow-developing power plays should be avoided. There can also be cohesion between offensive and defensive systems, as when a pressure or rebounding basketball defense supports a fast-break offensive system. The strategic systems should fit the program resources available for teaching and practice.

Language Systems

Every profession involves its own unique language. Whether medicine, the stock market, psychology, or sports, there is precise terminology and language to quickly describe and communicate the information necessary to efficiently make things work. Everything can be described in plain English, but not nearly as quickly or precisely.

The language of a profession includes general terminology, shortcuts (slang), and unique terms created within individual programs or staffs. General football terminology, most of the slang, and a multitude of operating concepts are readily available in football glossaries. The best of these is *The Smart Football Glossary* by Chris B. Brown, found at smartfootball.com. A team coach is responsible for developing the language system to be used by the team. It takes some thoughtful analysis of the program needs to choose how complicated the language needs to be and how it is going to be communicated. An entry-level program may have the coach on the field to call a play like right-half dive, while advanced teams may use a signal system to call, "Slot right, pistol, Z motion, 24." Remember that the program language should be recorded in some form and taught to everyone who is going to use it.

When working with the program language, it is important to remember that poor communication leads to mistakes. Avoid terms that sound the same, such as *keep, sweep,* and *sneak.* Avoid abstract terms that have no context or descriptive content, as they can be hard to remember. For example, do not use *razor* if it does not mean something to the right or a cutting pass route. Combine similar offensive and defensive plays in a series with a distinctive name like *24 belly, 35 counter,* or *goal line 8.* For more-complex systems, review all the terms involved to avoid duplication. For example, if *Sam* is the strong-side defensive safety and *Slob* is a stunt for the safety through the strong-side B gap, avoid short *S* words for defensive calls that do not involve the strong safety.

There are ways to upgrade even the simplest program language.

1. A quarterback wristband can contain ten to twenty selected formations and play combinations, or a small number of formations can be signaled together with a listed play number on the band. A separate wristband worn by a back or receiver could contain a list of numbered third-down or red zone plays, all of which can then be called in the huddle.
2. Defensive rotations, line adjustments, and stunts can be signaled with distinctive gestures.
3. If the pre-snap cadence has a place for an automatic change of the play, like *Blue 50* or *5 Oklahoma*, the quarterback can react to a defensive mistake by using a hot or automatic word. For example, if the middle linebacker covers motion and leaves the A gap open, the quarterback can use the hot call *Red* and the play number *10* (or *10 Ohio*) to change the play to a quarterback sneak. Xavier football once used a ferocious animal as their hot call. It almost backfired in laughter when *rhinoceros* was the only ferocious animal the quarterback could think of to use.

DEVELOP A PLAYBOOK

The playbook is the operational manual for the offensive, defensive, and kicking-game strategic systems used in the program. It should contain a list of everything the team plans to do in a game. When the playbook is completed, it will provide the basis of all teaching, skill requirements, and talent allocations for the team.

For entry-level programs, the offensive playbook should contain a series of plays for quick handoffs (dive), double-team blocks at the point of attack (power I, belly), fake-handoff play action (counters), basic drop-back passes (combinations of preset pass routes for each receiver), and quick passes (for low-risk plays or to take advantage of mistakes in defensive coverage). Running the same plays from a few different base formations adds sufficient variety to be unpredictable. More-advanced play series can address attacks at every gap, all play-action passes, all down-and-distance situations, responses to pressure, and special situations, such as goal line plays.

The entry-level defensive playbook should have only one or two base formations with man-to-man or zone pass coverage. Simple adjustments for the wide side of the field or the strength of the offensive formation and a few pressure plays should provide sufficient flexibility

When the offensive and defensive systems are selected, it is time to develop the plays to put the systems into effect. A play is a specific deployment and movement pattern for each possession or, in static sports like football and volleyball, each separate unit of a possession. Plays can be invented or selected from a vast array that have been used successfully to operate specific systems. For example, systems relying on speed will use plays that outflank or outmaneuver the defense.

Understand Play Design

With the numerous play designs available in books, on TV, and through playbook software, it is easy to overlook the fundamental elements of designing, teaching, and calling a play. Understanding these elements is the key to implementing all offensive and defensive tactics. Everything from scouting to communication to game plans will be easier. Even defensive plays, reads, and adjustments are based on understanding offensive play action.

Play design starts with identifying a situational objective based on down and distance, game clock, score, and/or momentum. For example, a play designed to gain one yard should work differently from one needed to gain long yardage. Although the design elements may have varying levels of risk in lost yardage, execution, and lost possession, those decisions are not addressed in play design but in play selection.

Movement

Every play has a movement plan for potential ball carriers or receivers. Even a simple quarterback sneak may have movement to fake a quick outside pitch, block into the line, or open a quick pass route. There are many standard movement patterns to choose from:

- convergence of backs at the point of attack
- placement of the quarterback under center or five steps deep
- crossing of one or more backs with the quarterback or each other
- unpredictable changes in the direction of movement
- delays in movement, such as drop steps, draw (fake-pass) action, or freeze (read) options
- pre-snap motion of one offensive back at regular speed or on the fly, and either into or away from the strength of the formation

Shifting from one formation to another is not an element of play design, because the shift is used for other purposes, such as reading the defense or forcing defensive mistakes in coverage. However, it is advisable to design some plays to take advantage of common defensive mistakes in reacting to pre-snap movement.

The choice of movement patterns can have varied tactical objectives, such as moving one or more defensive players, concealing the point of attack, exploiting defensive weaknesses, defeating pursuit, or confusing defensive read rules.

BALL EXCHANGE

Play design includes both the method for exchanging the ball as well as all fake exchanges. Handoffs can be direct or extended (ride) and inside, toward the line of scrimmage, or outside, away from the line of scrimmage. They can also be multiple among different backs. In addition to handoffs, the ball can be exchanged by pitches, shuffle passes, and longer passes. The movement pattern combined with the exchanges and fake exchanges form the heart of a play, but there are additional significant elements.

BLOCKING SCHEME

While offensive-line blocking schemes can consist of basic rules for specific defensive fronts, play design is more effective if the schemes are coordinated with the play action. This takes advantage of a wide variety of blocking techniques. For example, a sweep play may be more effective with reach blocks or pulling linemen, and power plays can employ double-team blocks. Both gap-control and point-of-attack blocking schemes can be accomplished with a variety of the following blocking techniques:

➤ direct one-on-one drive, screen, and reach
➤ cross (X) blocks with other linemen
➤ double-team with linemen or backs
➤ pulling to trap a defender or lead a ball carrier
➤ downfield blocks on second-level defenders
➤ protection blocks for pass plays or backfield action or to seal backside pursuit
➤ decoy blocks to influence a defender's read
➤ backfield blocks for pass protection, double-teams, and isolation plays
➤ release blocks for screens, draws, and backside defenders
➤ line splits between blockers that are varied for specific plays or deception

PLAY AREA

The area in which play movement takes place can also be varied. For example, a short yardage play can be run within one side of a formation, while other plays work better with movement across the whole formation. The play area used also effects the timing of play movements. For example, it takes a long time for a wingback to run to the opposite side of the formation. It should be noted that pre-snap motion or spreading the formation can be used to take a defender away from the point of attack without the need for a block.

PERSONNEL

Play design should be matched with appropriate personnel. For example, a quick-pitch sweep should use a fast halfback rather than a big fullback. Small backs should not be assigned to block big linemen. Plays can also be designed for specific personnel or personnel packages. The effectiveness of plays can be enhanced by examining

- ➢ the speed of ball carriers and pass receivers,
- ➢ the size of blockers for power plays,
- ➢ pass-catching skills for ends and running backs, and
- ➢ situation objectives, such as a goal line jumbo group of big players at most positions.

PLAY-SERIES CONSISTENCY

If play movement is converging blockers at the point of attack, then that movement should be consistent no matter which carrier gets the ball or which gap is attacked. If fakes are an element of the design, then every play in the series should look the same no matter which exchanges are faked. Similarly, a screen pass or draw play should be designed with specific pass-play movement and blocking to take advantage of defensive reads and reactions.

It is most manageable to group similar plays in a play series to facilitate teaching and communication and to exploit common tactical elements. The series should be arranged in a playbook, which serves as the operating manual for the systems used by the program. The groupings of common plays can contain a variety of tactical elements. For example, a series of quick handoffs directly into a gap will have plays for every gap, sometimes by different ball carriers and with different blocking schemes. A series of power plays or counteraction plays will have the same common elements.

One of the tactical elements inherent in many play series is the use of fake handoffs to disguise the actual ball carrier and gap to be attacked.

POST-SNAP READS

Play design can include changes based on the actions of one or more defenders *after* the play has begun. The following are some basic examples of this type of change:

- ➢ A simple option to keep or exchange the ball can be based on a single defensive-player reaction. The design leaves the target defender unblocked, and the exchange can be a pitch or short pass. A passer can have the option to run if an outside rusher gives up outside containment responsibilities.
- ➢ Multiple options can be run in series as defenders appear.
- ➢ Read options isolate a defender at a distance from the exchange with a movement pattern that forces a commitment to one direction or another.
- ➢ Run-pass options focus on a specific pass defender with both run-and pass-defense responsibilities, such as a cornerback covering a receiver in the flat while containing a rollout passer.
- ➢ Blitzes and defensive pressure can be anticipated by holding possible receivers in the formation for blocking assignments, adding alternative pass routes for quick passes, and planning possible changes in blocking for broken plays and scrambles.

Add Tactical Options to the Playbook

In addition to the strategy decisions reflected in the play series chosen for the playbook, tactical elements can also be added to each series. The surprises, deceptions, and devices that can be employed in offensive, defensive, and special-situation plays are limited only by the imagination. Even if specific variations are not added to entry-level playbooks, the coach should be prepared to introduce them when the opportunity arises. Advanced programs will have multiple variations for each series or situation, as well as special designs based on scouting reports.

OFFENSIVE TACTICAL OPTIONS

Enhance each play series to change the method of attack. For a run series, add play-action passes, and for a pass series, add draw plays and screen passes. These plays are more effective when they start out looking like the base plays that the defense expects to see. The more-advanced programs will have numerous designs available, such as middle screens, quick screens, and short blocking-back tosses.

Change from the base formation. It is obvious that a quick handoff series can be run from most formations. Changing formations is a tactic that makes it more difficult to predict the intended play, and it forces the defense to prepare for more formations while providing the offense with opportunities to exploit mistakes in defensive adjustment. It is possible to operate any play series from at least some different formations.

Add motion. Using a back-in motion or shifts in formation adds a different look to plays and forces defenses to quickly adjust to a new formation while giving the offense a preview of the defensive backfield coverage system. Motion can be into the formation or toward the sideline. It is amazing how many defenses fail to cover a motion back or choose to move a run defender out of position to cover the motion.

Add false reads. Even if the defense is not coached to read offensive play movement or does not rely on scouting, there are some basic reactions that can be taken advantage of. For example, a pass defender may not cover a pass receiver who appears to be blocking rather than releasing downfield. Linemen who pull out of line to block elsewhere on certain plays may be followed by a defender, leaving a gap open for easy attack. Advanced systems can design variations of standard plays to take advantage of the read principles of specific opponents.

Add trick plays. Using a trick play generates varied reactions.

Some coaches consider it junk offense, while programs like Boise State use more than one a game. There is an art to trick plays because they can result in losses of yardage and disruption of offensive momentum. When they work, they can quickly change the score and shake defensive confidence. A potential advantage of using a trick play is that once it is shown in a game, future opponents may divert practice time to prepare for it, and you have the opportunity to prepare subtle changes in the play to attack expected defensive adjustments. Simple examples are a novel formation, a silent snap between the center and quarterback, a handoff run tossed back to the quarterback for a pass, a quarterback sweep that turns into a short forward shuffle pass, or a pass receiver who appears to stumble before jumping back into a pass route.

A basic principle of some trick plays is surprise arising from doing something different from what the defense expects to see. For example, the old Statue of Liberty play starts out looking like a pass but turns into a reverse handoff to a wide receiver. Other examples are a fake fumble (fumblerooski), or the quarterback turning to the sideline in confusion while the ball is snapped directly to a running back. The more the surprise is sprung from what the offense normally does, the better the chance of success.

Add something new. Defenses can be surprised by formations or play action they have not prepared for. Having a few simple designs in the playbook provides an opportunity to try out new ideas while saving some surprises for future opponents. Formations like triple flankers and unbalanced lines are a good start. Play action, like options, quick passes, and jet sweeps, will get defensive attention and create opportunities for mistakes in coverage.

Change personnel. Changing the size or speed of players or the position they take in a formation adds tactical advantages to the play itself, such as running a sweep with a faster back or running short-yardage plays with the biggest possible blockers. Advanced programs will try multiple formations to match their best receiver against a slower defender. It is also possible to switch the positions in a formation between a wide receiver and a tight end to leave the faster receiver covered by a strong safety. These tactics place additional preparation pressure on defenses and can set them up for false reads.

Shift coverage levels. While a base defense may appear the same at the snap of the ball, linemen or linebackers can drop back in pass coverages to disrupt delay passes or provide underneath cover for curls and crossing routes. Similarly, defensive backs can move toward the line of scrimmage to cover run gaps or pressure the offensive backfield.

Shift gap coverages. There are multiple options for gap responsibility in the 4–3 and 3–4 defenses to address offensive talent, formations, and down-and-distance situations. Having these adjustments in the playbook makes it more difficult for offenses to set blocking schemes and adds flexibility to the defense.

Use robber coverages. Zone and man-to-man pass coverages can be modified to free a pass defender from basic coverage responsibilities to jump and disrupt an expected offensive route. For example, a weak-side safety may cross under a deep receiver while the weak-side corner drops into safety responsibilities (invert), or an inside linebacker may move outside to defend a slant pass. Such moves not only disrupt the read and timing of the pass play but also provide the opportunity for interceptions. They are helpful in predictable passing situations and to take away the offense's favorite pass plays.

Slant to the field or formation. The direction of the line charge can be angled toward or away from the wide side of the field or the strength of an offensive formation. This can be done separately or in conjunction with linebacker movement and is effective in disrupting blocking schemes or meeting strength.

Add pressure plays. Both penetrating and reacting defenses can put pressure on running and passing plays by sending one or more defenders into the offensive backfield. Overpowering gaps, shooting gaps, and looping around blockers can all be employed in a wide variety of combinations. They are most effective when run from the base defense the offense is expecting to see, but there are advantages to showing the pressure in advance because the offense may try to change out of their chosen play or fail to properly address the threat. The pressure deployments can also become false keys.

Change personnel. Changing personnel to meet specific situations is also effective for defenses. At early levels of competition, substituting players to change size or speed avoids the need to change from the base defense. Combining these changes with some pressure plays can meet a wide variety of defensive situations.

IMPLEMENT STRATEGY AND TACTICS

Once strategic plans are prepared, it is time to decide how to put strategies into practice. This requires a shift from strategic planning to operational planning and is an intense process of decision-making to produce the schedule of activities for the entire season. The goal is preparing the team to execute the strategic systems effectively. This goal is achieved by designing the lessons that the players and team will be taught and fitting the lessons into the available time and resources.

Strategy-related subjects to be taught include the playbook, the position skills necessary to execute the system, the terminology required to efficiently communicate the system, and coordinated team movements. Each subject needs a baseline starting point and a planned sequence for achieving competence. For example, teaching the playbook can start with a base formation and a basic play series. Regular assessment, rather than a preset schedule, should control the pace of teaching because some teams learn more slowly than others and some subjects prove more difficult than anticipated. Each lesson should be coordinated with the others, so the formation, play movement, terminology, and position skills are taught at the same time.

Advanced programs can add strategic subjects such as pre- and post-snap reads, variations of position skills and techniques, situational awareness, and complex communication systems. Teams can also be taught how to practice and prepare for games through the season.

Several factors will impact the teaching schedule. The most important is the number of teachers available. If there is only one coach without volunteer support, it will be difficult to break down lessons for position groups, and more time must be spent in team sessions. Older or experienced players can lead tightly planned breakout sessions, and players can rotate through three activities practiced at the same time until everyone has had a turn at each activity. Observing the players who keep the group on task will identify team leaders, and watching the teachers is also a good way to assess their learning and mastery. The first team can also teach. For example, when the first-team offense has learned a new play series, they can switch to the defensive side and teach the second team to walk through the series. This frees the coach to focus on individual players or assess the progress of learning.

Determine the amount of homework that may be permitted by league or academic regulations. Much of the playbook can be studied as a text in advance of each practice session. Even if traditional homework is limited, you can have players watch college players who play their position or operate familiar strategic systems. Simply focusing attention on the TV-game analysis discussions will improve sports IQ and enhance the comprehension of whatever lessons are being taught in practice.

Identify the students for each subject to be taught—that is, which players will be in the offensive, defensive, and special teams classrooms on the field. This is not a simple matter of listing names on a chart. One of the reasons Jim Harbaugh achieved early success when he began to coach at Michigan was his ability to move talented players into the best positions to support his strategic systems. If players are unknowns at the start of the season, then use early drills and assessment to decide the matter.

The final factor that can impact the teaching schedule involves the last step in learning to execute the strategic system: full-team coordination in gamelike conditions. The number of times the starting (first) team can practice each play is a limited, precious resource. There is no substitute for the experience gained in full-speed communication, timing, and reaction to teammate and opponent movement. (One of the keys to the success of the University of Connecticut women's basketball team is running most practice activities at full speed.) The method for providing this experience to second-and third-team players varies, and there is no easy answer. If player numbers permit, the second team can gain a good deal of game experience in scrimmage sessions or reserve games with league opponents, and if fortune smiles, the second team can be played late in games with a comfortable lead. Increasing the first-team experience of more players involves the concept of reps, the number of plays practiced or played by individual players. This is a critical requirement to develop experienced substitutes for first-team players who are taken out of play by injury, equipment issues, or illness. The method for the sequence, timing, and recording of player reps should be planned for practice and games. If there is no assistant to control the process, individual players can be responsible for getting their reps under planned substitution procedures.

Plan the Practice Schedule

Even if there are no regulations to limit available practice time, player stamina, concentration, and family schedules always impose practical limits that should be respected. Therefore, plan the number of possible practices for preseason (two a day if permitted) and then the number of practices between games during the season. Allocate time for the following practice elements in each preseason practice: warm-ups (initial sessions should include instruction and explanations); conditioning, speed, and agility exercises; individual position instruction and drills; offensive, defensive, and special teams coordinated formations; communication and playbook instruction (for programs with limited staff, most instruction may have to occur in these sessions); contingency time for unexpected action, such as depth-chart evaluation and changes, correction of performance errors, catch-up instruction, rules, strategy, and team-cohesion issues such as discipline and behavior; team administration time, such as travel, equipment, and schedules; and postpractice wrap-up or locker-room time.

Once the practice segments are identified, develop a lesson plan and goals for each segment. Identify the leader, the pupils, the lesson goals, and the drills and equipment to be used. If there are multiple small groups involved, the assigned practice area should be listed.

The same process can be used for in-season practices, except the teaching elements can be changed to include review of scouting reports, skills required in the game plan, playbook and tactical adjustments in the game plan, special situations, and special teams. These items do not have to be addressed at each practice; for example, you can cover skills and scouting early in the week with team coordinated activities later in the week.

Develop a Game Plan

Before starting practice to prepare for an opponent, turn the strategies for defeating the opponent into a game plan for offense, defense, special teams, and special situations. The game plan serves in part as a lesson plan for teaching the plays, adjustments, and skills that are required to execute the plan. The game plan is also a practice plan to focus on correcting mistakes and confusion and to refresh execution of everything that may be used in the coming game. These aspects of the game plan can be as detailed as resources permit, ranging from formations to blocking schemes or gap coverages to individual player techniques and matchups. The game plan for each opponent should also include any seasonal strategic plans for adding new plays and showing specific plays to set up future opponents. (Advanced strategic systems include a plan to reveal new play variations each game with the intention of forcing future opponents to commit more practice time to preparing for the variations, and the playbook includes subtle adjustments and tricks that are saved for use against specific future opponents.)

The key to successfully executing a game plan is preparation. Watching a game is like watching a courtroom TV show, where there is no indication that a trial lawyer may have spent days reviewing hundreds of pages of testimony and other documents to prepare for one hour of questioning. The details of a game plan are developed in practice. Preparation creates confidence, and as Peyton Manning says, "Pressure is something you feel when you don't know what the hell you're doing."[12]

When the details have been addressed and the plan is made, it is time to let go of the details and let the universe—the Almighty, fate, chance—take over. Things very seldom happen as planned, and sticking to the plan in the face of changed circumstances, or "sweating the details," rarely leads to success. From some of the

---

[12] Hand, *Defensive Coordinator's Football Handbook*, 234.

greatest battles in history to games we see on TV every week, the ability to adapt and stay focused on the goal is the path to victory.

OFFENSIVE-PLAN PRIORITIES

- ✓ organize plays by down and distance
- ✓ identify formation changes from base
- ✓ organize plays by anticipated defenses
- ✓ separate pass plays by zone or man coverage
- ✓ list available blocking adjustments
- ✓ develop backup plan for key injuries
- ✓ list plays to attack defensive coverage and alignment mistakes

DEFENSIVE-PLAN PRIORITIES

- ✓ organize base defense, blitzes, and pressure plays for down and distance, red zone, and special situations
- ✓ list available pass coverages and backfield rotations
- ✓ list gap coverage adjustments
- ✓ list opportunities to exploit offensive-formation weaknesses

SPECIAL-SITUATIONS PRIORITIES

- ✓ organize goal line and fourth down plays
- ✓ prepare a two-minute offense and defense
- ✓ list adjustments for various weather conditions
- ✓ plan a trick play list, including fake-kicking plays for offense and defense

CHAPTER 5

PRACTICE DEFINES PLAY

MAKE A PLAN FOR IMPROVEMENT.

For every hour of game play, a team spends at least five hours in practice. But it is not the amount of time that matters; it is how that time is spent. Every minute of practice is precious. The level of conditioning, skills, discipline, and execution seen in a game reflects how well the team has practiced and how the coach has used the available practice time.

Using practice time efficiently is a critical coaching skill. It requires a combination of teaching (lesson plans), management (resource allocation and organization), strategy (goals of practice activities), and leadership (team identity). As overwhelming as this may appear, the steps to success involve very manageable planning and operation.

PRACTICE SCHEDULE

Whatever time is available for a specific practice session should be divided among the following activities:

- individual skills (optional time for skill positions and a chance for all players to try out their abilities)
- warm-up
- skills and conditioning
- execution by position (alignment and individual position movement)
- offensive-team activities

- defensive-team activities
- special situations
- kicking game and transitions in possession
- team meeting

The allotted times can vary from one practice to another. For example, during two-a-days, the afternoon session may spend more time on teaching and less on conditioning, or the practice before a game may emphasize team coordination and game plans. Depending on the number of staff, each time slot can be further divided among specific position groups or among first-and lower-level players.

When each segment is in the schedule, develop a lesson plan for each. The plans can be as simple as warm-ups led by team captains to a play list for run-throughs and timing. It is important to have a goal for each segment and to keep a record of progress. For example, teaching the skills to run a sweep play may require more time than practicing the basic skills, and it may be necessary to plan a future segment to achieve the lesson-plan goal.

Stick to the schedule. Whatever happens in a segment, whether injuries, unplanned issues, or unmet goals, it is critical to stay on schedule. It is better to lose a segment than disrupt the entire schedule. It is also important to maintain a disciplined routine that does not tolerate delays and wasted time.

Evaluate every segment. While routine activities may develop a sense of order and confidence, they can be an opportunity for complacency. Even warm-up and skill reviews should have goals of maximum effort and concentration. Raising the performance level of all the players in the group is also a measurable goal. Many coaches are eliminating the term *drills* because it does not connote a constant drive for improvement.

Evaluation sets the goals for the next session and maintains a steady learning curve. It can also provide the inventory of strategic opportunities, such as additions to the play lists and emerging talent. Attention should also be paid to the development of team dynamics and sport IQ.

Address weaknesses. It may be fun to practice the things that work well, but weaknesses need to be improved and mistakes eliminated.

If the competition scouts opponents, every weakness may be attacked in future games. When addressing any weakness, it is necessary to determine the cause of the problem. For example, causes can include lack of effort, poor skills, lack of talent, lost concentration, or a poorly designed assignment.

Instill values. Mike Singletary, Chicago Bears Super Bowl championship linebacker, said, "Before we can talk about a championship, we have to practice like a championship team." If practice is only a repetition of what was done before, there will be no improvement. The quality of the time spent in practice is controlled by the values brought to practice. The coach and team should consider and commit to the following list of values every time they step into the practice area:

- Improvement. Strive to do everything better, faster, and longer than the time before. This value is driven by a focus on assessment (both self-assessment and external assessment) and teaching.
- Focused attention. Learn to focus 100 percent on one exercise, one play, one lesson at a time.
- Safety. Understand the conditioning, skills, resources, and situations that can reduce injuries.
- Teamwork. Work as a team on and off the field.
- Playing smart. Learn the game and the keys to victory.

TURNING AROUND A LOSING TEAM

Some teams need to experience losing before they can learn what it takes to win. Moving forward after a loss is a character-building experience. However, some teams and programs are mired in a losing culture. Whether the result of poor coaching, overmatched competition, or a dearth of talent due to attrition or injury, a losing culture is sustained by a losing attitude that is quick to find a reason to lose or give up. The signs of a losing attitude are reflected in the way a team approaches everything they do. Changing attitude begins with changing behavior.

Being alert to losing behaviors is advisable after any loss, as it is the foundation of teaching a team to behave and play like winners. In his book *Above the Line,* Urban Meyer focuses on the line of performance that separates average from elite. Before a team can get to excellence, they need to focus on improving the performance of everything they do. Here is a list of behaviors to strive for:

- ❖ Take care of appearance and equipment.
- ❖ Be on time, and hustle everywhere on the field.
- ❖ Eliminate goof-off behavior and distracted attention. You can assign sprints after practice for the offenders so no time is taken away from practice.
- ❖ Recognize extra effort and hustle.
- ❖ Repeat activities until they're done right. I observed a team practice in which three punts were blocked. The coach did not take the time to fix the problem, and sure enough, that team had a punt blocked in the next game.
- ❖ Focus practice activities on success. This idea is often referred to as going back to the basics. Review techniques and put a stopwatch on everything from kick coverage to pass protection and pass routes. Set up success every day by doing more than the day before, whether in terms of endurance, speed, mistake-free repetitions, pop quizzes, or positive team time. Use dummies or blocking pads for lessons rather than live player-versus-player contact.
- ❖ Eliminate limits and excuses by focusing on challenges and solutions.
- ❖ Build a cohesive team in practice and on the field by providing every player with a sense of personal improvement and a role in achieving team success. Regularly give every player a chance to lead warm-ups and demonstrate new techniques.

Since success in early-level programs is determined primarily by coaching, it is necessary for the coaches to take some hard looks at what they are doing. The first thing to assess is whether the practices are focusing on the winning behaviors addressed above. Next is a full evaluation of the coaching strategies to determine what is working and what is causing problems. Review the talent and execution needs for the strategies that are being used. Solve problems by making appropriate adjustments. For example, use double-team blocks to support a weak lineman, use quick-hitting run and pass plays for a weak line, or use line splits and zone blocks. On defense, look for slants and stunts to cover weak points.

Finally, evaluate the risk levels of the offensive and defensive systems being used. Reduce turnovers and become less predictable by throwing on first down and using more screens and reverses. On defense, blitz on first down and mix up pass coverages, or try shifting fronts before the snap. Play to the score, and do not take risks with field position. You can make your team more difficult to prepare for by adding a new special formation like double wing or unbalanced line. You can also rework the kicking game to improve field position, and you can increase turnovers by installing better rush plays on punts. Use a quick kick on third down, and practice corner and sideline kicks. Reduce the risk of mistakes and lost gambles. Practice the kicking game with the same coaching effort as devoted to offense and defense. Stop the run, and defend the middle of the field.

THOUGHTS FOR A NEW COACH

For coaches entering a multi-coach program, the focus is simple: know your responsibilities, work for the team, and learn everything you can.

Coaches in the head-coach position for the first time should focus on living each day as the type of coach they want to become. Before any planning, take time to look and listen. Assess the team and the program for strengths and weaknesses, starting with the fundamentals of conditioning, skills, and talent. Know the resources that are available to the program. Then assess the competition to determine the level of competitiveness, focusing on what needs to be done to beat the best teams on the schedule.

Values. Keep the system simple. Make practice fun and rewarding. The Positive Coaching Alliance reports that 70 percent of young athletes quit organized sports by age thirteen because they are not having fun.[13] Distribute success. Mistakes are learning experiences. Improve every day.

Personal tasks. Know the rules and teach them. Scout. Know the reason for each play call. Watch momentum. Watch the clock. Keep opponents guessing and on their heels. Prepare for everything from equipment to game plans to substitutions. Maintain discipline and routines.

SCOUTING

No strategy is better than a gamble if the opponent's plans are unknown. I was fortunate to play for a coach who used a scout team of volunteers together with game film of every opponent we faced. Years later, I volunteered to scout for a local high school team and was shocked to find that the coach rarely obtained opponents' game film and did not believe in showing his players any scouting information. In competitive team sports today, scouting can encompass most of the legal aspects of detection, assimilation, deduction, and deception developed by military intelligence. The key difference is that a sport program has limited resources to gather information and limited capabilities to use it. An effective scouting system should be designed to fit the program in which it is used.

The first step in designing a scouting program is to understand the power of scouting and how it is accomplished. Whether the head coach is the only scout or will be teaching a scout team, start by reading *Football Scouting Methods* by Steve Belichick. Steve, the father of Bill Belichick, the New England Patriots Super Bowl coach, spent his career scouting for Navy. Although the book is somewhat dated in its focus on the running game, it provides a thorough foundation in this critical coaching skill.

Scouting preparation begins with identifying the information that is needed. Too much information can be as worthless as no information at all. It is also counterproductive to gather information that cannot be used at the team's level of execution.

---

[13] "Mission Statement," Positive Coaching Alliance, accessed October 3, 2017, http.//www.positivecoach.org/about/mission statement.

Scouting information starts at a very general level and becomes an increasingly more detailed collection of statistics, subtle adjustments, and individual player talent and techniques. The type of strategic information available varies among offensive, defensive, and special teams, including just about every special situation that can be imagined.

The amount of information that can be gathered is dependent on the personnel available, their experience and training, and the relevance of the scouted game to the systems your team uses.

Finding Information

The difficulty in gathering information lies in the discipline and understanding required to obtain accurate and complete data. A scout should know two things: what to look for and how to recognize it when it appears. These skills apply whether scouting for a business to buy, a route to take, or a restaurant to try. First and foremost, the information is not for the scout; it is for the person or program that needs the information.

In team sports, the scouts need to understand the systems and strategies used by offensive, defensive, and special teams. If the team being scouted is passing against man-to-man coverage and the scout's team rarely uses man coverage, there is no sense trying to detail all the man pass routes. (Note that the scout must first recognize the difference between man-to-man and zone pass coverage.) If the defense being scouted is playing against a spread offense and the scout's team does not use a spread offense, the defensive adjustments and rotations being used against an empty backfield do not provide much useful information. If the scout cannot report observations in the language system used by the team, most of what is reported will be of little value.

Knowing what to look for starts with knowing what you are looking at. A good scout should quickly recognize both offensive and defensive formations, alignments, and play systems commonly used by team opponents. The scout then needs to quickly record the information observed on the field in an understandable form. *Defensive Coordinator's Football Handbook* by Leo Hand explains how to do this for both offenses and defenses. The book also discusses scouting reports and provides a detailed list for gathering opponents' tendency information.

If the head coach does not have a competent scout or scout team, he or she should do the job personally by whatever means and time are available. At the entry levels of competition, there are practical opportunities to scout. A recording of an opponent's game is the most reliable and efficient source of information. Recordings can be viewed at any time and can be viewed multiple times to obtain detailed information. Even an amateur recording by a parent or friend is better than sending an untrained person to attend an opponent's game. Multiple recordings of each opponent can provide additional information if they are permitted by league rules.

The following are some alternative ways for a single coach to obtain basic scouting information:

- Observe future opponents when they are playing at a convenient time.
- Have a volunteer or friend record games.
- Watch opponents' pregame warm-ups.
- Observe opponents during your own team's games.
- Talk to coaches who have played future opponents.
- Obtain rosters and numbers for the opponent players.

OFFENSIVE SCOUTING INFORMATION

- general offensive system used (spread, power, option) with pace, line set, and snap cadence
- base formation(s) and QB position
- strategic design of offense, such as speed, misdirection, or power
- each play run with gain or loss
- red zone plays
- trick plays
- down and distance for each play
- key personnel

DEFENSIVE SCOUTING INFORMATION

- base defense
- standard pass coverage (zone or man-to-man, and two or three deep safeties)
- pressure or read-react system
- defensive front alignment
- big plays surrendered (ten-plus yards)
- red zone defense
- blitzes and linebacker stunts used
- safety rotation to wide side of field or strength of formation
- key personnel

SPECIAL TEAMS SCOUTING INFORMATION

- kickoff lineup and coverage
- kick receiving lineup and return play
- punt formation
- punt defense, rush, and return strategy
- kick receivers
- speed and flank protection

If a scout team is available, the members should be trained and organized. The more the scouts understand the strategic and tactical elements involved in their team's systems, the more useful their information will be. Fortunately, there are multiple products available for recording information. They range from basic paper forms to complex, computer-coded data that can be sorted and searched with almost unlimited flexibility. For example, it is possible to retrieve an opponent's punt time from snap to kick and compare it to your team's best rush time. A selection of scouting materials is provided in *Football Scouting Methods* and in the list of additional resources in this book.

Even at the most basic level, try to obtain a written scouting report. Committing a report to writing produces more detail and better organization, and the document will be available for quick reference. Always make notes of clarifications, strategic analysis, and additional questions.

Use Scouting Information Strategically

Before the scouting report is presented to the team, there should be a game-plan meeting between the coaches and the scout team to discuss the available information and to outline strategic plans for the next opponent. Obviously, if there are no scouts, the coach will be responsible for designing and implementing the game plan, but the scouting review process is a key in obtaining every advantage from the available information.

Scout-team meetings have tremendous, subtle advantages. First, these meetings provide recognition and job satisfaction to the scouts. Second, they offer evaluation and refinement to the scouting system. Third, the coach can obtain personal impressions and information not presented in the written scouting report. Finally, working as a collaborative team is a joint learning process taking advantage of creative synergies, increased comprehension of strategic information, and more efficient communication among the coaching staff. The result of this process is that wonderful feeling of "I know what you're thinking."

Scout-team meetings have two goals. The first goal is to analyze all available information to determine the opponent's strategic intentions in regard to their offensive, defensive, and special teams as well as special circumstances. This involves a mental shift from focusing on *what* the opponent does to *why* they do it. For example, does the opponent use triple flankers to spread the defense for more-open inside runs, to overload zone pass coverage, or to take advantage of fast receivers? The second goal of the meeting is to decide on the strategic response to the opponent's threatened actions. For example, if the use of triple flankers is to run inside, the defensive line can slant to the strength of the opponent's formation or use stunts to disrupt run plays. If the flanker threat is an overload on the pass defenders, the defense can switch to man coverage, rotate a linebacker into the zone, or pressure the passer.

Finally, maintain a scouting file indexed by opponent, strategic systems involved, and the game plan used. If a coming opponent runs a single-wing offense, there are advantages in quickly finding historic scouting information on running and defending that system.

GAME DAY

The magic of game day begins hours or days before a game, when floating anxiety appears and thoughts keep turning to the game. The time leading up to a game is a time for self-doubt for players and coaches. Players wonder, *Will I perform to my best?* and coaches worry, *Have I done enough?* The goal of a coach on game day is to restore and maintain the team's confidence. The coach achieves this goal by planning the game-day activities to address the physical, mental, and emotional components of preparing for athletic competition.

The coach can meet players' physical needs with injury protection and prevention, nutrition and hydration, and adequate warm-up activities. Next, by reducing distractions and providing clear, organized reviews of the game plan and goals, the coach can foster mental alertness and focus. Finally, the coach should assess the team's emotional state to determine the best psychological atmosphere to achieve a balance between calm confidence and competitive excitement.

Game day should be planned to eliminate distractions, assure that everyone involved is ready to do their job, and provide the team with a routine for preparing to play. The planning process focuses on listing necessary preparations and deciding on the schedule for team activities. For the preparations, it is best to start with the team support needs and list everything from transportation and meeting space to equipment and nutrition. Setting the schedule is easier when working backward from kickoff time.

Preparations Checklist

The coach should delegate responsibility for as many tasks as possible, even if volunteers are used. Everyone with delegated tasks should report to the coach for questions and to confirm completion of his or her assignments.

1. Pack all uniforms and support materials for transport to game.
2. Arrange game-time support: equipment, training supplies, communications, medical, and weather items.
3. Confirm any transportation arrangements.
4. Transport game-plan materials.
5. Check location of all team meeting areas.
6. Set sideline positions for special teams, substitutions, skill position warm-up area, messengers, and signalers.
7. Set plans for field conditions, sideline safety areas, and security if necessary.
8. Outline for meeting with game officials.

Game-Day Schedule

Set a written time for each necessary team activity and allow for sufficient time to complete the activity. It is important to stay on schedule and to make any adjustments as soon as a delay occurs. Plan the schedule by starting with the kickoff time and working backward through the following activities.

✓ Final run-on before kickoff. Warm up, have final meetings, and set up communications.
✓ Locker-room time before run-on. Check equipment, update game plan based on opponent warm-up and substitutions, plan kickoff or return, and have pregame talks.
✓ On-field warm-up. Perform team and individual warm-ups and skill activities, and run through plays. Set up support areas for program personnel, check field and weather conditions, and observe opponent personnel for substitutions. A critical task during this time is a meeting with the game officials. Get to know each official personally, and find out each official's background and experience. While all officials want to do a good job, it is appropriate to discuss their points of emphasis and how they will enforce rules on sportsmanship, blocking techniques, and pass defense. Alert them to any trick plays or formations that the teams may use,

and point out any potential rules violations you anticipate the opponent making. For entry-level competition, officials may provide help in educating all players about the rules. During the game, it is appropriate for the coach to question officials about the rules (rulebook reference), the basis for specific calls, and the consistency of application. Officials have the last word on judgment calls, and there is nothing a coach or player can do to change that, although coaches can request before a game that officials discuss some judgment-call situations with each other on the field before making a final call.

✓ Locker room (assembly area). This is the time for dressing, assembling equipment, taping and managing injuries, and having focusing talks. Some teams send skill players out early to warm up without pads.

✓ Arrival time for the game. Add travel schedule if applicable.

✓ Unexpected delays. Plan for the unexpected. In a program segment about Alabama coach Nick Saban, ESPN described college football's decision to postpone games for dangerous weather conditions in the interest of player safety. Alabama was one of the first teams to experience such a game delay. When the team left the playing field and returned to the locker room, Saban had already prepared in advance; he had a list for how to handle the postponement, including team activities, nutrition, coaches' meetings, and a warm-up schedule for returning to the field after the delay.

Coach's Personal Plans

It is helpful for the coach to set a personal schedule for game day, starting with a review of all game-time plans, including all plans for coaching and staff responsibilities, equipment and supply needs, and possible weather issues. Prepare or review all pregame and halftime talks with the team. Review and confirm any pregame travel arrangements and any postgame transportation and nutrition plans. Take some time to visualize flawless execution of the game plan.

Sideline Presence

Every coach has a personal choice of his or her role during a game. There are several factors to consider in making this choice:

- ❖ Team personality. Does the team need a cheerleader, a calm focus, a field general, or a motivator?
- ❖ Time priorities. Determine the tasks that should be accomplished first, such as play calling, substitutions, injury management, special teams, clock and momentum management, and game-plan adjustments.
- ❖ Sportsmanship. A coach's sideline behavior is an example for the team and the program. Emotional control, respect for players and officials, and good sportsmanship in the face of victory and defeat should be taught by example at every opportunity.

CHAPTER 6

TAKE THE FIELD, COACH

SAVOR THE CHALLENGE AND FIND THE MAGIC FOR YOU AND YOUR TEAM.

THE LURE OF TEAM SPORTS

Becoming a team coach can appear overwhelming. The highest-level coaches make huge salaries and spend most of their lives dedicated to the profession, but they do not do it for the money. Look at how many coaches and players delay retirement until long after their financial future is secured. The passion and will to continue are found in the lure of team sports, an activity that reduces competition, hard work, personal growth, and personal satisfaction to their purest levels in the context of a team of brothers or sisters working toward a shared goal under a leader who inspires them to be the best they can be. The lure is a lifetime of magical memories—from the songs that were sung, to living in the world of the game, to the joy of reaching a goal. *Magic* is the right word, because the moments cannot be controlled or scripted; they appear as each player—and the team itself—evolves.

At the start of one undefeated high school football season, we were tied by a tough opponent. As we entered the locker room after the game, there was no yelling, anger, or speeches, just crying. When the coach came into the room, he looked around and said something simple like, "Let's go home and get back to work." The next week, in a game against a favored opponent, we scored the first six times we had the ball. No one ever talked about going undefeated, but everything we did as a team had that unspoken goal. At the end of the season, it was not the victories that mattered but those magical moments when we'd worked, played, and laughed as one.

As you assume the position of coach, remember that it is not a job but an adventure. Teaching becomes easy when you focus on the students and look for the moments when they get it. Never use the word *drills*; enjoy the success of every technique and play during practice. Pick your strategy to fit your style and your team, without worrying about what anyone else will think. View each game as a personal challenge to become immersed in the action and take charge of the contest.

A coach's anxiety on game day is focused on whether he or she has adequately prepared for the game. Called butterflies, stage fright, or just game-day jitters, this anxiety is the personal challenge to finding the magic of coaching. Trust your preparation by quickly resolving unexpected issues while staying focused on executing your plans. Concentrate on the team during pregame activities, and become a field general during the game. Make decisions by relying on your values rather than the pressures of the moment.

Win or lose, the magic is in giving your players experiences, lessons, and memories that they will remember for the rest of their lives.

BIBLIOGRAPHY

Abrashoff, Michael D. *It's Your Ship: Management Techniques from the Best Damn Ship in the Navy.* New York: Warner Books, 2002.
Innovation can occur anywhere. This is, perhaps, the best practical guide published on building teamwork.

Bass, Tom. *Youth Football Skills and Drills.* New York: McGraw-Hill, 2006.

Belichick, Steve. *Football Scouting Methods.* New York: Ronald Press Company, 1962.
This book has been criticized as outdated, but it remains the best source available for scouting methods and issues. The focus on a 5–2 defensive front still has application for entry-level strategy.

Bolton, Robert, and Dorothy Grover Bolton. *People Styles at Work.* New York: American Management Association, 1996.
A workplace guide to understanding people and building relationships.

Brown, Daniel James. *The Boys in the Boat.* New York: Penguin Books, 2014.

Burnett, Darrell. *It's Just a Game!* New York: Authors Choice Press, 2001.
Written by a child psychologist, this guide for parents of young athletes discusses youth sports and self-esteem.

Chopra, Deepak. *The Soul of Leadership.* New York: Harmony Books, 2010.
Dr. Chopra offers a metaphysical understanding of the dynamics between groups and their leaders. His thoughts take the development of leadership systems to a higher level. If you are interested in Eastern philosophy, read or listen to anything by Dr. Chopra.

Clark, Bobby. *Baffled Parent's Guide to Coaching Youth Soccer*. New York: Rugged Mountain Press, 2000.

Dorfman, H. A. *Coaching the Mental Game*. Dallas: Talor Trade Publishing, 2003.

In this book, Dorfman, a sports psychologist, focuses on how to develop the mental team traits that can lead to team success. The A-to-Z list of traits provides a wealth of insights for developing a personal leadership style.

Dougherty, Jim, and Brandon Castel. *Survival Guide for Coaching Youth Football*. Champaign, IL: Human Kinetics, 2010.

Ehrmann, Joe. *InSideOut Coaching*. New York: Simon & Schuster, 2011.

A wonderful focus on the essence of coaching. The Ohio Interscholastic Athletic Administrators Association has founded an InSideOut educational program based on this book.

Ferrigno, Vance. *Training for Speed, Agility and Quickness*. Champaign, IL: Human Kinetics, 2000.

Flores, Tom, and Bob O'Connor. *Coaching Football*. Chicago: Masters Press, 1993.

A very good beginner's guide to becoming a total coach, from strategy to scouting and game adjustments. Reference chapter 20, "Planning Strategy," and chapter 21, "Strategy Checklists," for a review of scouting information and preparation of a game plan. Chapter 22, "Making Game Adjustments," and chapter 24, "Preventing Injuries" are also quite useful.

Gallwey, W. Timothy. *The Inner Game of Tennis*. New York: Random House, 2008.

A great start to understanding the science of neuromuscular learning and the miracle of muscle memory, which somehow transfers learning to new cells. (Think about riding a bike years after all the cells in your body have been replaced.)

Gilliam, Joe W., Sr. *Coaching Football's Multiple Formations Offense*. Monterey, CA: Coaches Choice Books, 2000.

Gwynne, S. C. *The Perfect Pass*. New York: Scribner, 2016.

A wonderful read that explains strategic innovation through the passion of a struggling coach.

Halberstam, David. *The Education of a Coach*. New York: Hachette Books, 2005.

In this book, noted author Halberstam describes the life and development of Bill Belichick, the Super Bowl champion coach of the New England Patriots.

Hand, Leo. *Defensive Coordinator's Football Handbook*. Monterey, CA: Coaches Choice, 2015.

A must-read for every football coach! Chapter 1, "Contemporary Offensive Overview," details the evolution of offensive theory beginning in the early 1900s, and the rest of the book is an example of the strategic complexity in college-and professional-level sports.

Holtz, Lou. *Wins, Losses, and Lessons: An Autobiography*. New York: HarperCollins, 2009.

Coach Holtz was selected three times as college football's National Coach of the Year. He continues to present his personal style as a life coach and motivational speaker. Read and listen to anything by Coach Holtz.

Hybels, Saundra, and Richard L. Weaver II. *Communicating Effectively*. New York: McGraw-Hill, 1986.

In its fourth edition, this book remains a textbook introduction to the art of personal communication and public speaking.

Ivey, Patrick. *Complete Conditioning for Football*. Champaign, IL: Human Kinetics, 2012.

Jones, Renwick. *Let Them Play*. Bloomington, IN: iUniverse, 2012. Solid information on teaching youth-league players from all backgrounds.

Kirby, Alex. *The Big Book of Saban: The Philosophy, Strategy and Leadership Style of Nick Saban*. Self-published, CreateSpace, 2017.

Coach Saban, who coached in college and the pros, has developed Alabama into one of the top football programs in the country.

Lipton, Bruce H. *The Biology of Belief*. Carlsbad, CA: Hay House, 2005.

Read this book to exercise your mind, understand physiology, and learn how human cells communicate with each other and the world.

Lombardi, Vince. *Vince Lombardi on Football*. New York: Galahad Books, 1973.

A primer on football with glossary, photos, and diagrams for key plays and every position.

Meyer, Urban. *Above the Line*. New York: Penguin Press, 2015.

Advice on leadership and team building from Urban Meyer, the 2015 national championship coach. This book explains Coach Meyer's leadership system for team sports through his own personal philosophy and concepts. It provides a framework for all other reading that is available.

National Research Council. *How People Learn.* Edited by John D. Bransford, Ann L. Brown, and Rodney R. Cocking. Washington, DC: National Academies Press, 2000.

National Strength and Conditioning Association. *Essentials of Strength Training and Conditioning.* Champaign, IL: Human Kinetics, 2016.

Quinn, Ronald W. *Ethical Coaching.* US Youth Soccer Workshop.
Quinn is an associate professor in the Department of Sport Studies at Xavier University and is also a US Youth Soccer National Instructor.

Renner, Bill. *Communicating Plays in a No Huddle Offense Using Numbers.* Self-published, CreateSpace, 2015.

Shanahan, Mike, and Adam Schefter. *Think like a Champion.* New York: HarperCollins, 1999.
Coach Shanahan twice took the Denver Broncos to a Super Bowl championship.

Schembechler, Bo, and John U. Bacon. *Bo's Last Lessons.* New York: Hachette Book Group, 2007.
In this book Bo Schembechler, the legendary coach of Michigan, teaches the timeless fundamentals of leadership.

Shapiro, Robert M. *Dare to Prepare.* New York: Three Rivers Press, 2008.
How to use planning as a key to success.

Sugarman, Karlene. *Winning the Mental Game.* Burlingame, CA: Step Up Press, 1999.
A practical guide to team building and mental training. Forget what you think you know about teamwork and player attitudes. This is the in-depth foundation for all coaches.

Sun Tzu. *The Art of Strategy: A New Translation of Sun Tzu's Classic, "The Art of War."* Translated by R. L. Wing. New York: Doubleday, 1988.

USA Football. *Better Safer Game.* Monterey, CA: Coaches Choice, 2015.

Vaughn, Dean. *How to Remember Anything.* New York: St. Martin's Griffin, 2007.

Walsh, Bill, and Brian Billick. *Finding the Winning Edge.* Champaign, IL: Sports Publishing, 1998.

Two very successful NFL coaches focus on how to manage for success. Chapters 3, 4, and 5 discuss the role of a head coach, a successful organizational structure, and how to organize the staff.

Zukav, Gary. *The Dancing Wu Li Masters.* New York: HarperCollins, 2001.

Read this book to exercise your mind and learn about the transition from Newtonian physics to quantum physics.

ADDITIONAL RESOURCES

American Football Coaches Association (AFCA). Professional development committee. https://www.afca.com

American Youth Football (AYF). Provides *The Huddle* newsletter and rulebooks. https://www.americanyouthfootball.com

CompuSports. Football coaching software. https://www.CompuSports.com

Coach's Office. Football software. https://www.CoachsOffice.com

Cramer Sports Medicine. Offers a full line of athletic training and treatment products. https://www.CramerSportsMed.com

Foundation for Safer Athletic Field Environments (SAFE). Sports Turf Managers Association. Safety checklists. https://www.SAFEFields.org

Hudl. A product and service of Agile Sports Technologies that offers tools for recording and uploading game video to make playlists and automated reports for game plans. https://www.Hudl.com

Just Play Sports Solutions. Coaching tools to build interactive playbooks, scouting reports, and quizzes. https://www.JustPlaySolutions.com

Krossover. Provides game-film breakdowns for team sports with custom playlists and highlights. https://www.krossover.com/about/

National Alliance for Youth Sports (NAYS). 2050 Vista Pkwy., West Palm Beach, FL 33411. https://www.nays.org

National High School Athletic Coaches Association. (NHSACA) https://www.hscoaches.org

National Strength and Conditioning Association (NSCA). Bookshop. Certification and a full range of topics in bookshop. https://NSCA.com.shop/books

National Athletic Trainers' Association. Offers online education in sports safety: ConcussionWise, environmental emergencies (lightning, fluid replacement, heat exhaustion), general medical management (diabetes, etc.), sport safety management, pediatric overuse, emergency preparedness (spinal, cardiac). https://www.NATA.org

Pop Warner Football (PWF). Coaching certification clinic. https://www.PopWarner.com

Positive Coaching Alliance (PCA). Now supported by Fox Sports. https://www.positivecoach.org

USA Football. A must-see source for player safety education! https://www.USAFootball.com

Youth Football Coaches Association. Free drill library and coaching certification program. https://www.yfbca.org

Printed in the United States
By Bookmasters